QUADRILLE PUBLISHING   PHOTOGRAPHY BY TOBY GLANVILLE

Stevie Parle's
DOCK KITCHEN COOKBOOK

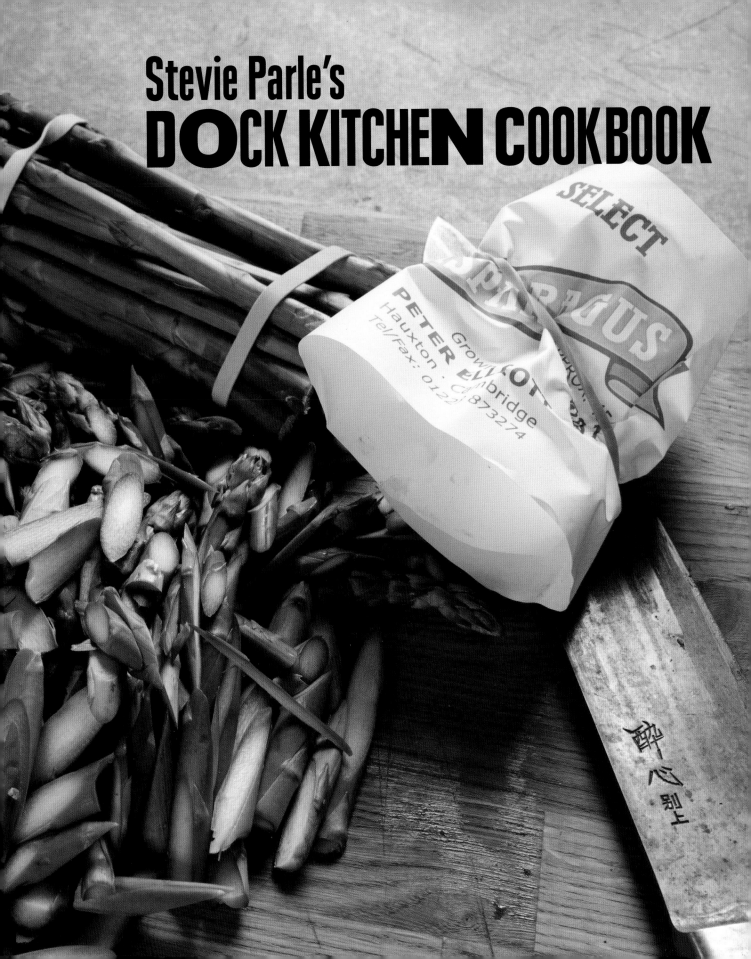

Editorial Director Anne Furniss
Creative Director Helen Lewis
Project Editor Lucy Bannell
Art Direction & Design Lawrence Morton
Production Director Vincent Smith
Production Controller James Finan

First published in 2012 by
Quadrille Publishing Limited
Alhambra House, 27–31 Charing
Cross Road, London WC2H 0LS
www.quadrille.co.uk

Text © 2012 Stevie Parle
Photography © 2012 Toby Glanville
Design and layout © 2012 Quadrille
Publishing Limited

Cataloguing in Publication Data:
a catalogue record for this book is
available from the British Library.

ISBN 978 184949 116 7

Printed in China

INTRODUCTION

Though I am still young, I do not think it is rash to say that you never stop learning to cook. As both a professional and a home cook, it is still very exciting to eat new things; the satisfaction of recreating a dish I first enjoyed somewhere exotic back home in my kitchen in London is quite remarkable.

My restaurant Dock Kitchen came about more or less by accident. It was to be a pop-up, a slightly longer-lived temporary restaurant in a series of one-off events I was holding in London. But there was something about it I couldn't let go. The building deserved a restaurant that would stick around: the long canal-side Wharf structure, an ex-Victorian goods yard with a massive terrace, was just too perfect to abandon. I needed a more permanent home to develop my cooking. I wanted a place to show people the exotic, simple recipes I had found around the world and adapted into a style that has more to do with the cooking of the grandmothers of the globe than the overworked, fussy food of the average London restaurant. Dock Kitchen is a restaurant about cooking, always simple, often exotic, with carefully sourced, honest ingredients. The food, though sometimes unfamiliar and largely foreign, seems to sit well in London, the most multicultural of cities; perhaps this inclusive approach is the new Modern British cooking.

When you meet really good cooks, or cooks you feel will become really good, you can tell that they have all made the same important discovery. That cooking for someone is a very special thing. It is a simple but many-layered act of caring and love, protection and respect that is hard to communicate in any other way. Even giving someone a piece of toast and a cup of tea is a way of showing you are looking after them and care about their well-being. I try to communicate this emotional side of the act of cooking in my restaurant. Most of the dishes are home cooking of one form or another from one place or another and, though we may serve 200 people a day, many of them strangers, I like to think they leave feeling as comforted, nourished and cared for as if they had been guests in my home.

A certain amount of greed is to be expected of a good cook. I am always surprised to meet chefs that hardly eat anything, or never go out to eat. Knowing how to enjoy a good meal is very important if you are going to be able to cook a really good meal for others. I often think of someone, "they really know how to eat" and, generally, "they really know how to cook" leads on from that.

Curiosity seems to be another important factor. Good cooks all seem to be curious. Some are curious about technique: a lot of restaurant chefs have become obsessed with new ways of cooking, and so water baths, dry freezers, distillers and liquid nitrogen bottles are becoming the everyday tools of some modern restaurant kitchens. Others are curious about history and the cultures that have spawned the great dishes of the world. For me, a collection of mortars and pestles, some ancient cooking vessels, charcoal ovens and unusual home recipes collected from around the globe are where my curiosity takes me. I find them significantly more exciting than any of the gadgets and gizmos to which many chefs seem to aspire these days.

Cooking is about confidence. I remember early on in my cooking career seeing the late Rose Gray, perhaps the best cook I have known, cook a piece of wild salmon. She threw Maldon salt on to the flesh with startling confidence, then chucked it on the chargrill and grilled it over the hottest coals for a matter of seconds. The fish was well-charred on the outside yet raw inside. She spooned her well-loved chilli and olive oil on to the piece of fish and put it on the pass. All in an instant. She was so confident that the salmon was delicious, so sure of herself that it needed a good amount of salt, that the flesh was best rare and that it would be improved by chilli, that she didn't think about any of it. It just happened. Cooking really is not hard, especially if you know your ingredients well.

This book tackles quite a lot of ingredients that in the past have been fairly difficult to find, but can now be found on the corner of almost every street. Though many of us seem to be still scared of them.

These days, ingredients that 20 years ago could only be found in specialist shops, such as good olive oil, even garlic, are an irreplaceable part of the British diet. There's no reason for us not to develop the same everyday comfort around pomegranate molasses or cardamom... I just want to speed the process up a little.

A lot of good cooking is in good shopping. Enjoy it. Seek out interesting ethnic shops, talk to the owners, buy something you don't recognise and find out from them what it is and how to cook it. Learn from the knowledge of your butcher and fishmonger, or the stallholder at your farmers' market. Become familiar with the exotic ingredients all around you and soon you will find yourself reaching for tamarind as easily as you do balsamic vinegar. Your cooking will be all the better for it.

Whenever I am travelling I always go to markets, even when I am staying in a hotel and wouldn't be able to cook anything anyway. I always find it fascinating to watch people choose food, particularly the grannies, they really know what they are doing. You can learn that a small, straight finger of okra is better than long, that medium-sized green chillies are the ones to choose, or not to pick courgettes that have gone a bit bulbous at the end.

It's easy to tell good produce. Great vegetables look like they are not long from the veg patch. They can be knobbly and muddy; we are not looking for the perfect shapes and boring uniformity that supermarkets specify, but instead for the rough beauty of lovingly grown produce.

Good meat is dry with lots of fat, spices are whole and green if they should be green, brown if they should be brown, never dusty or broken. A fresh fish looks bright-eyed and sparkly. In short, beautiful-tasting ingredients are beautiful to look at, which makes it easy for a good cook.

SPRING

This simple and delicious soup is a favourite among staff and customers. The spice mix is warming and exotic and works perfectly here, but it is also great used to season a piece of slow-roast or grilled meat. If you haven't got the Baghdad Bharat (and why not? The recipe is on page 182), put in a pinch of coriander, a little cumin and turmeric and a scratch of nutmeg.

IRAQI WHITE BEAN SOUP

SERVES 4

olive oil

1 red onion, finely chopped

2 large celery sticks, finely chopped

2 tbsp Baghdad Bharat (see page 182)

1 small bunch of coriander, stalks and leaves separated and finely chopped

sea salt

250g canned whole plum tomatoes, washed of their juice

2 x 400g cans of cannellini beans, rinsed

Heat a generous amount of olive oil in a heavy-based saucepan. Fry the onion and celery with the spices, coriander stalks and salt for about 30 minutes. As always this long, slow frying process is very important to give flavour to the whole dish.

Add the tomatoes and continue to cook, breaking them up a little with the back of your wooden spoon. Add the white beans and enough water to give a consistency you like (don't use too much) and continue to cook for 10 minutes more. Adjust the seasoning and stir through the coriander leaves. Serve with chunks of crusty bread.

This is a kind of *sopa de tortilla*. Usually based on a tomato broth, this one has loads of greens; just use whatever you can get, ideally you want a good mixture. In Mexico they have all kinds of herbs we don't have. You can get some of them dried from coolchile.co.uk.

MEXICAN GREEN SOUP

SERVES 6

2 small sweet red onions, roughly chopped

1 small heart of celery with leaves, roughly chopped

2 garlic cloves, green sprouts removed, cut into chips

large pinch of dried oregano

1 tsp ground allspice

2 green chillies

olive oil

2 litres of chicken stock

1kg greens (a mixture of chard, spinach, borage, nettles, fenugreek… whatever you have), shredded into ribbons

corn oil, to deep-fry

6 small corn tortillas, cut into 1cm strips

1 avocado, finely chopped

250g fresh cheese (I use ricotta, though a proper cottage cheese or junket would be nice too)

lime wedges, to serve

Fry the onions, celery, garlic, oregano, allspice and whole green chillies in a large, heavy-based pan with a good glug of olive oil. Fry for about 10 minutes on a medium heat, stirring occasionally, then add the chicken stock and bring to a boil.

Once the broth is boiling, add all the shredded greens. Boil fast for about five minutes.

Meanwhile, heat a medium pan with a 2.5cm depth of corn oil until almost smoking hot. Fry the tortillas quickly until crisp, then put on a plate lined with kitchen paper.

Spoon the greens and broth into bowls and top with the avocado, cheese and the fried tortillas. Serve with wedges of lime.

When we can, we use cocum at Dock Kitchen. It is a dried fruit similar to a mangosteen and lends a beautiful smoked taste to fish curries. If we can't get cocum (it's hard to find, we have to send someone to a south Indian shop), we use a block of tamarind instead.

HOT AND SOUR RED MULLET AND CLAMS CURRY SERVES 4

2 tbsp flavourless oil (I use mild olive oil)

handful of fresh curry leaves, picked from stems

1 tbsp ground coriander

¼ tsp fenugreek seeds, ground

1 tsp mustard seeds, ground

1 tsp mild (Kashmiri) chilli powder

2 red onions, thinly sliced

sea salt

5cm fresh root ginger, finely chopped

500g can whole plum tomatoes, washed of their juice

6 pieces of cocum, or 50g block of tamarind, soaked in 200ml boiling water

2 x 300g red mullet, each cut into three through the bone

250g carpet-shall (palourde) clams, well washed

Choose a medium, heavy-based saucepan and heat the oil. When hot, add the curry leaves. As soon as they crackle add the other spices, then immediately the onions. Season with salt, reduce the heat and add the ginger. Let the onions cook for about 20 minutes until soft and sweet.

Tip in the tomatoes and continue to cook slowly, letting the flavour develop gradually. Add the cocum, or mush up the tamarind and add the liquid/pulp through a sieve.

Add the pieces of mullet and the clams, cover and cook for about five minutes, until the fish pulls easily from the bone and the clams are open.

Toasts are often a starter at Dock Kitchen, though they vary with both season and whim; you'll find other versions for each season in this book. I try to choose one toast with great umami (in this case olives), another with great freshness (here broad beans) and the last earthy and rich (chickpeas). I use a southern Italian loaf called *altamura*, made with semolina. Any good, open-crumbed, chewy sourdough bread would work.

THREE LITTLE TOASTS FOR SPRING: CHICKPEAS, OLIVES AND SMASHED BROAD BEANS

SERVES 4

For the toasts

good olive oil

4 large slices of coarse sourdough bread

For the olives

100g small, firm black olives

1 anchovy fillet

1 scant tsp salted capers, soaked

leaves from 1 sprig of thyme

½ garlic clove, green sprout removed, crushed in a mortar and pestle

For the chickpeas

400g can of chickpeas, rinsed

1 garlic clove, green sprout removed, crushed in a mortar and pestle

pinch of dried wild oregano

1 dried chilli

For the broad beans

½ garlic clove, green sprout removed, crushed in a mortar and pestle

a few leaves of mint

a few leaves of marjoram

100g small, sweet broad beans

1 tsp finely grated parmesan, or to taste

squeeze of lemon

For the olive toasts, stone the olives, then chop them with the anchovy, capers and thyme. Mix with the crushed garlic and stir in enough olive oil to moisten.

To make the chickpea topping, heat the chickpeas with a bit of fresh water, the garlic, dried oregano and chilli. Once the garlic has cooked, smash everything up with a wooden spoon, then mix, pouring over enough olive oil to make a thick, earthy, slightly spicy, rough paste.

For the broad bean toasts, keep the garlic in the mortar then add the herbs and smash again. Add the broad beans and bash everything about with the pestle. Mix in the parmesan, then stir in olive oil to moisten. Finish with a squeeze of lemon just before you use it.

Toast the bread on a cast-iron griddle pan until dark and crunchy and cut each piece into three. Spread each of the toppings thickly on four of the toasts.

A thoran is a fast-cooked south Indian dish. We make a lot of different thorans at Dock Kitchen; there's one for every season in this book and there are countless more. This asparagus version works very well.

ASPARAGUS THORAN

2 tsp flavourless oil (I use mild olive oil)
1 tsp brown mustard seeds
small bunch of fresh curry leaves, picked from stems
4 large mild dried chillies
1 bunch of asparagus, chopped into 1 cm lengths
sea salt
½ coconut, flesh peeled and finely grated

In a wide pan or large frying pan, heat the oil until almost smoking. Add the mustard seeds and, when they crackle, the curry leaves and dried chillies.

A few seconds later, tip in the asparagus, season with salt, then cook for a few minutes until the asparagus is just soft. Stir in the coconut. Serve with White or Brown Chapati (see page 183).

We vary these lovely little pizzette as we like, sometimes with treviso (the best kind of radicchio) and a strong soft cheese, or with thinly sliced fresh tomatoes, dried oregano and chilli.

These delicious versions with lardo are my favourite. Lardo is back fat from large white Italian pigs. It is salted in marble baths for about a year and has a delicious, delicate, fatty taste.

PIZZETTE BIANCHI

For the pizzette

1 tsp dried yeast

200ml warm water

250g strong white bread flour, plus more to dust

20ml olive oil

For the topping

2 large waxy potatoes, peeled

2 sprigs of rosemary

2 garlic cloves, green sprouts removed

olive oil

sea salt

freshly ground black pepper

12 paper-thin slices of lardo di colonnata

First make the dough: mix the yeast with a little of the water and a pinch of the flour and let this sit for about 10 minutes to come alive. Mix this yeast mixture with the olive oil and the remaining flour and water in a large bowl. Knead for around five minutes to produce a glossy, loose dough. Cover with cling film and leave to prove for an hour in a warm place.

Meanwhile assemble the other ingredients. Slice the potatoes paper-thin (use a mandolin if you have one). Pull the needles from the sprigs of rosemary. Very thinly slice the garlic and put it in a dish, then cover in olive oil.

Roll the dough into four balls, place them on a tray lightly dusted with flour and leave them for another 30 minutes, covered in cling film.

Preheat your oven to its highest temperature (300°C/570°F is ideal, though only achievable in a commercial oven!), putting in a heavy metal tray or pizza stone to heat up.

Roll out the dough balls on a lightly floured surface into 2mm thin discs. Top each with a few slices of potato, some of the rosemary and a few slivers of garlic. Season with salt and pepper.

Place each pizzetta directly on to the tray or hot pizza stone; bake for about four minutes until crisp and lightly brown. Lay the slices of lardo on the pizzette as they come out of the oven and eat immediately.

We use bottarga or salted anchovies to make this unusual and delicious plate. It is essential that all of the herbs and leaves are really fresh, best is when they come straight from your window box or garden.

Sometimes at home when I can't be bothered to make flatbread, I toast a bit of pitta from the shop; it's not nearly as good but only takes a second.

LABNE, BOTTARGA, PICKLES, RAW VEGETABLES, HERBS AND SUMAC

SERVES 4–6

½ tsp fenugreek seeds, ground

1 tsp sea salt

250g thick Greek or Middle Eastern yogurt

20g bottarga, or 8 salted anchovy fillets

a little sumac

good olive oil

large plate full of herbs and leaves, whatever looks good: mint, tarragon, parsley, purslane, dill, holy basil, Italian basil, marjoram, oregano, lamb's lettuce, tiny spinach or chard leaves...

4–6 Yeasted Flatbreads (see page 185)

4 carrots, cut into long sticks

2 small cucumbers, cut into long sticks

8 pickled green chillies

To make the labne, add the fenugreek and salt to the yogurt, then spoon it into a coarse woven tea towel or muslin cloth. Tie it up and hang or let sit in a sieve at room temperature for a few hours, with a bowl underneath to catch the whey.

The rest of this recipe is really assembly.

Spread the labne on to a large plate, grate over the bottarga (or finely chop and sprinkle over the anchovies), sprinkle with sumac and pour on a bit of olive oil. Pile the herbs and leaves on a big plate – eliminating any bruised or brown leaves – and sprinkle with a little water.

Roll out the flatbreads and bake them in the hottest oven (we cook them in the tandoor) or over a grill or barbecue.

Put the raw vegetables and pickles on another plate. Encourage people to wrap a bit of labne and herbs in a flatbread with a pickle and a bit of carrot or cucumber.

This is a lovely little salad. Sometimes we add pan-fried sweetbreads to it which is really delicious, but totally changes the dish. Choose artichokes with tight heads that look very fresh.

ARTICHOKES WITH PRESERVED LEMONS

8 small or 4 larger artichokes

small bunch of thyme

1 head of garlic, plus 1 small garlic clove, green sprout removed

1 lemon, halved

sea salt

1 preserved lemon, thinly sliced

1 tbsp black olives, roughly chopped

1 tbsp blanched almonds, roughly sliced into thin slivers

4 tbsp really good olive oil

1 tsp cardamom seeds, finely ground

1 heart of celery with leaves, finely chopped

4 tbsp thick yogurt

Peel off the artichoke leaves from the base until the leaves are paler green and tender about halfway up their length. Peel the dark green part from the stalks then cut the tips of the leaves off at the point where the leaf becomes tough. Remove the furry choke inside with a little spoon.

Put the artichokes, thyme, head of garlic and lemon in a saucepan, cover with water and season well with salt. Put a small plate into the pan on top of the artichokes to keep them under water. Bring them to a boil and then simmer gently until the stems are soft; this could take five to 30 minutes depending on the size of the artichoke.

Make a mixture of the crushed garlic clove, preserved lemon, olives, almonds, oil, cardamom and celery. When the artichokes are cooked, add them to the mixture.

Spread a plate with the yogurt and top with the artichoke mixture. Enjoy on its own, or with a little fresh flatbread or toasted pitta.

I'm always happy to see the first elderflowers and was delighted to come across a version of this recipe in Patience Gray's brilliant book *Honey from a Weed*. It's excellent to be able to do some other things with elderflowers, as they grow everywhere and most people only make cordial with them. Pick your elderflowers on a sunny day, as they will taste better. These are brilliant with a glass of prosecco.

ELDERFLOWERS IN GRAPPA BATTER

SERVES 4

100g plain flour

25ml grappa

200ml ice-cold sparkling water

flavourless oil, to deep-fry

16 elderflowers

Sift the flour into a mixing bowl. Add the grappa, then slowly pour in the water, mixing as you go; you are aiming for a thin, light batter about the consistency of pouring cream. Dip in your finger: the batter should coat it but not so thickly that you can't make out your fingernail.

Heat the oil to 180°C/350°F in a deep-sided saucepan or deep fryer. Dip the flowers in the batter, knock them against the side of the bowl to remove any excess, then deep-fry until crisp, light and just starting to brown lightly. Drain on kitchen paper and serve immediately.

Ragoût is a perfect way to use the abundance of amazing vegetables in the spring, though the gluts of other seasons are used to good effect in three more ragoûts in this book. Don't worry that the vegetables lose their colour, as their taste will change and improve with the long cooking time. You could add artichokes or spinach, spring morels or samphire.

RAGOÛT DE LÉGUMES SPRING

2 small red onions

½ small head of spring garlic

1 head of celery with leaves

50g unsalted butter

5 bay leaves

a few sprigs of thyme

1 bunch of asparagus, chopped into short lengths

500g small sweet peas, podded

400g small sweet broad beans, podded

100g new potatoes

sea salt

1 bunch of agretti, soft shoots picked from tough brown stalks, or other bitter greens such as chicory

a few sprigs of parsley, dill, mint and marjoram, leaves picked from stalks

Finely chop the red onions, the spring garlic and the outer layers of the celery with a bit of the leaf. In a large, heavy-based pan, fry the chopped aromatics in the butter with the bay and thyme.

After 15 minutes or so, when all is soft and sweet, add the celery heart, cut into new potato-sized pieces, and the asparagus. Braise for a few minutes, then add the peas and broad beans. Meanwhile, boil the potatoes in well-salted boiling water until just soft, then add to the mixture in the pan with the agretti.

Splash in a bit of water, put on the lid and stew gently for 15 minutes until everything is soft and delicious. Roughly chop the herbs and stir through the ragoût.

We make quite a lot of pilaf at Dock Kitchen: aubergine in the summer; cauliflower in the winter. It's a great dish to be able to make as the variations are endless.

SPRING VEGETABLE PILAF

200g white basmati rice

1 red onion, thinly sliced

75g unsalted butter

1 tsp allspice berries, ground

½ tsp ground cinnamon

1 tsp cardamom seeds, ground

1 small bunch of asparagus, tough stems snapped off, spears roughly chopped into the size of broad beans

200g fresh small peas, podded

200g fresh small broad beans, podded

sea salt

freshly ground black pepper

a few sprigs of parsley, dill and mint

4 tbsp thick yogurt

big pinch of sumac (optional)

Wash the rice very well, then soak it in plenty of warm water for two hours. In a medium pan with a tight-fitting lid, fry the onion gently in the butter with the spices for 15 minutes or more, until soft, sweet, and well broken down. Add the asparagus, peas and broad beans and season well. Let the green vegetables cook for about five minutes until well-flavoured and beginning to soften. Increase the heat to frazzle them a bit, then add the rice.

Meanwhile, boil a kettle of water. Stir the rice mixture gently, then pour over the boiling water up to 2cm above the level of the rice. Taste the hot liquid for salt. Cover with a piece of greaseproof paper and the lid. Cook on a high heat for three minutes, then on a low heat for six minutes, then remove from the heat. Leave the rice to sit for 10 minutes, undisturbed, for the grains to gain a little resilience, so they separate when served.

Mix the herbs through the rice, serve with yogurt and sprinkle with sumac, if you have some.

THE IMPORTANCE OF INDIA

India is one of the great food cultures of the world. Its cuisine is so diverse that it infuriates me when we demote everything to 'curry'. In the UK it seems that Indian food is not truly valued. Having grown up in Birmingham, I am all too familiar with the strange fare that passes for Indian in most curry houses.

At Dock Kitchen and at home I cook lots of Indian food. Strangely, people associate it with cheap restaurants. I use the same tomatoes and wild sea bass in a *cacciucco alla Livornese* (Tuscan fish stew) as I do in a hot and sour fish curry, yet people view the latter as being of less value. A strange kind of prejudice...

Most modern, glamorous Indian restaurants seem to feel they have to echo Michelin star-driven French restaurants in terms of style and presentation. The result is that there is no restaurant in the UK that I know of serving excellent home-style Indian cooking with the best-quality ingredients. No one has opened the River Café of Indian food... perhaps one day I will do it myself.

I adore proper Indian food and cooking it is always a joy. It is genuinely regional, perhaps because, in India, there are more people still living where they were born, so the food retains its local colour. Recipes vary from town to town and state to state. Many of the differences are determined by the ingredients of each region.

In the south of India much of the food is characterised by the use of coconuts – they grow everywhere – and a predilection for fish or vegetables over meat. In the North the main media for cooking are curd (yogurt) and ghee, while other dairy produce such as paneer (fresh cheese) is common. Of course it's more complex than that, but these key ingredients do make a big difference.

Religion also plays a big part. Each community has its own rules and traditions governing diet.

The north of India has a strong Moghul influence and the food has a definite Persian feel, biriani being the most obvious example. Biriani is a real celebration of a dish, often finished with gold leaf, vibrant pomegranates, cashew nuts, boiled eggs and sweet herbs. It's up there with bouillabaisse, bollito misto and Singaporean devilled crab as one of my Great Dishes of the World. The north of India also has a wealth of flatbreads, often cooked in a charcoal tandoor or on a dry pan above a little paraffin stove. As you travel around India you get a feel for local tastes: Gujarati food is somehow sweeter, the spices a little more delicate; in Bengal you find searingly hot river fish curries; in Karnataka delicious dosas (pancakes made from fermented rice and lentils). India is the most fantastic place to explore food, the diversity and enthusiasm of the cooks is really inspiring.

This Catalonian recipe first caught my eye because of its extraordinary name. A beautiful saffron-laced fish stew, it is baked in the oven with a picada of almonds, garlic, saffron and parsley. Picada is a useful tool, a way to add punch, usually with raw garlic, sometimes paprika or almonds. Zarzuela is also the name of an operetta or a variety show in Spain; I imagine the name comes from the many kinds of fish in the stew.

CATALONIAN FISH STEW WITH MUSSELS (ZARZUELA)

SERVES 6

500g monkfish tail

1 small red onion, roughly chopped

½ small heart of celery, roughly chopped

olive oil

2 bay leaves

2 sprigs of thyme

1 tsp paprika *piccante*

400g can of whole plum tomatoes, washed of their juice

200ml white wine

50g coarse breadcrumbs

2 garlic cloves, green sprouts removed

sea salt

a few sprigs of parsley

pinch of saffron

50g blanched almonds (preferably Spanish)

1 red mullet, filleted

400g wild bass fillet, cut into 4 pieces

200g small, clean rope-grown mussels

If it hasn't already been done by your fishmonger, pull the skin from the monkfish: you should be able to do this with your hands and the occasional nick with a sharp knife to help you on your way. Cut the fish through the central bone into four pieces.

Fry the onion and celery in a heavy-based pan in olive oil with the bay leaves, thyme and paprika. After about 10 minutes, once the vegetables are soft, add the tomatoes, increase the heat and add the white wine. Simmer for 20 minutes. Preheat the oven to 200°C/400°F/gas mark 6.

Meanwhile, make the picada. Fry the breadcrumbs in a generous splash of olive oil until golden and crunchy. Crush the garlic with salt, parsley and saffron, add the almonds and pound until coarsely ground. Add the fried breadcrumbs and set aside while you assemble the dish.

Place the monkfish, red mullet and bass in an earthenware oven tray and pour over the tomato sauce. Add a little water and the mussels, then sprinkle over the picada. Bake in the hot oven until the fish is easy to flake apart and the mussels open (about 15 minutes).

Serve with a plate of greens or potatoes liberally dressed with olive oil and sherry vinegar.

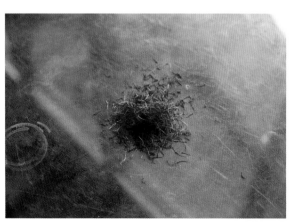

This Venetian classic may seem a bit wintry with polenta, but it's made lighter by finishing the polenta with olive oil, not butter and cheese. Find a good coarse polenta, preferably white.

CRAB, CLAMS, BROWN SHRIMPS AND RED MULLET ON WET POLENTA

SERVES 4

100g white polenta (not quick cook)

olive oil

1 garlic clove, green sprout removed, thinly sliced

1 dried chilli, crushed

½ tsp fennel seeds, roughly crushed

1 medium (300g) red mullet, filleted, each fillet cut into 4

20 small carpet-shell (palourde) clams, well washed

½ glass of white wine

1 whole tomato from a can, washed of its juice, torn into small pieces

150g crab meat, white and brown

100g brown shrimps

a few sprigs of parsley, roughly chopped

Cook the polenta according to the packet instructions. When it is ready, whisk in enough olive oil to give a pleasingly smooth, though not oily, consistency.

Heat a large frying pan, splash in a little olive oil, add the garlic, then the chilli and fennel seeds. Put in the red mullet and fry for a few seconds, followed by the clams, wine and torn tomato. Follow these with the crab and shrimps, cooking quickly until the clams are open and the crab is soft. Add the parsley.

Spoon the polenta on to plates and top with the fish mixture. Drizzle with a little extra olive oil. Drink soave.

You can roast the bass whole, fillet and bake in the oven, or grill on a barbecue or chargrill, it will be good however you cook it. With a rich gratin like this, try to cook the fish quite dry, without wine or too much oil. Herbs such as rosemary or bay are always welcome. Large, wild, line-caught sea bass are incomparable to the small, flabby, farmed specimens.

GRILLED SEA BASS WITH CHARD GRATIN

SERVES 6

sea salt
2kg chard
1 lemon
6 garlic cloves, green sprouts removed
50g unsalted butter
1 tbsp plain flour
250ml whole milk
freshly ground black pepper
100g coarse white breadcrumbs
8 anchovy fillets
1 x 3kg sea bass
olive oil

Boil a large pan of well-salted water. Strip the chard leaves from the stalks and cut the stalks into 1cm strips. Blanch the leaves until soft, remove from the pan and lay out to cool. Squeeze the lemon into the water and add the chard stalks (this will stop them from discolouring). Boil the chard stalks until soft, about 10 minutes. Drain and lay the stalks out to cool.

Crush the garlic cloves with some coarse sea salt until completely smooth. In a large, wide pan, heat the butter over a medium heat. Once it begins to foam, add the crushed garlic. When the garlic has begun to cook and the smell has filled the room, add the chard leaves and stalks then sprinkle over the flour and cook, stirring, for about three minutes. Slowly add the milk, still stirring; you should have a thick, glossy, pungent mixture, season well with salt and pepper.

Transfer the chard mixture to a baking tray, sprinkle over the breadcrumbs and lay over the anchovies.

When you are ready to eat, preheat the oven to 200°C/400°F/gas mark 6. Bake the gratin for 20–25 minutes until well-browned and hot throughout.

Meanwhile, fillet the bass and cut into 180–200g pieces. Season them well, moisten with a little olive oil then cook over a very hot charcoal grill, or in a very hot cast-iron chargrill pan, for about three minutes on each side, until a roasting fork inserted into the flesh feels no resistance. Serve with the chard gratin.

I have recently become slightly obsessed with *mastiha*, or gum mastic. My understanding is that it is the sap of a tree, tapped in a similar way to rubber and left to dry into 'pearls' of sap. *Mastiha* is often used to flavour sweet recipes, or as a stabiliser in ice cream. I was alerted to its use in savoury cooking by a blog post by food writer Anissa Helou (anissas.com).

CHICKEN ROASTED IN MASTIC AND POMEGRANATE MOLASSES WITH BRAISED BROAD BEANS

SERVES 6

½ tsp gum mastic

½ tsp cardamom seeds

1 tsp allspice berries

2 tbsp pomegranate molasses

salt

1 large handsome chicken, off the bone

1kg broad beans in the pod

2 tbsp olive oil, plus more for the chicken

3 garlic cloves, green sprouts removed, cut into little chips

freshly ground black pepper

4 ripe tomatoes, or 400g can of whole plum tomatoes, washed of their juice and torn or roughly chopped

small bunch of coriander

Preheat the oven to 200°C/400°F/gas mark 6. Grind the mastic with the cardamom and allspice to a fine powder. Rub the spices, pomegranate molasses and some salt into the chicken and lay him out on a large roasting tray.

Chop the bean pods into 3cm lengths, discarding the ends. Heat a heavy-based pan over a high heat. Pour in the olive oil, followed by the broad beans and the garlic, season well and add the tomatoes. Reduce the heat and cover the pan with the lid, but leave it slightly ajar. Cook for about 30 minutes, until very soft.

Drizzle the chicken with a little olive oil and roast for 20–30 minutes, until the flesh is no longer translucent. Just have a look, it's easy to tell as the bird is off the bone. Roughly chop the coriander and stir it through the broad beans, then serve with the chicken.

Biriani is one of the great dishes of the world, it takes a long time to make but is worth it. It is a dish you find all over India and it's interesting to see how the spices change in different regions. Rabbit is not a classic, but the delicate, distinct flavour of good-quality farmed rabbit is perfect in this most delicious of Indian celebratory dishes. Sometimes we add gold leaf and, if you make it in winter, you can sprinkle it with pomegranate seeds.

RABBIT BIRIANI

450g basmati rice

sea salt

2 red onions, thinly sliced

5cm fresh root ginger, finely chopped

150g unsalted butter, ghee or olive oil

4 tsp garam masala

¼ tsp turmeric

1 tsp ground ginger

1 tsp coriander seeds, ground

1kg farmed rabbit legs (about 4 hind legs)

250g thick yogurt, plus more to serve

150g blanched almonds, coarsely chopped

1 tsp black cumin seeds

20 green cardamom pods

3 star anise

1 cinnamon stick

8 black cardamom pods

pinch of saffron

fresh or dried rose petals (optional)

leaves from 1 small bunch of coriander leaves, roughly chopped

Soak the rice in warm water with a good pinch of salt for at least an hour. Then wash it until the water runs clean.

Choose a pan with a thick base, a tight-fitting lid and high sides, big enough to accommodate both meat and rice. Fry the onions and ginger in the butter, season well with salt, then add the garam masala, turmeric, ground ginger and coriander seed.

When the onions are soft and sweet, add the rabbit and cook for a few minutes to brown a little and absorb the flavours, then tip in the yogurt and nuts. Pour in about 250ml of water and cook gently over a low heat, covered with a piece of baking paper, until the rabbit is well-flavoured and quite soft. This will take about one hour.

Drain the rice and mix with the remaining whole spices. Soak the saffron in a few tablespoons of boiling water. Put the rice mixture on top of your delicious rabbit curry and cover with boiling water to just 2cm over the level of the rice. Season with salt. Increase the heat to high for the first few minutes, then low for the next 10. Remove from the heat and leave undisturbed for at least another 10 minutes.

Splash the saffron water over the rice. Garnish with fresh or dried rose petals, if using, scatter some coriander on each plate and eat with yogurt.

SUMMER

When it's in season, there is nothing better than sweetcorn. It's great to find a few things to do with it after you have eaten your fill of barbecued or boiled whole cobs with butter. Removing the corn from the cob is strangely satisfying. Epazote is a wild herb found all over South America. It tastes a bit like tarragon, with a slight flavour of anise and almost a smell of petrol. You can get chipotle adobo from coolchile.co.uk. It's a kind of chilli jam.

SWEETCORN AND SMOKED CHILLI SOUP WITH CRÈME FRAÎCHE

SERVES 4

6 sweetcorn cobs

1 red onion, finely chopped

2 garlic cloves, green sprouts removed, thinly sliced

1 sprig of tarragon (or dried epazote leaves), chopped

¼ tsp ground allspice

1 tbsp light olive oil

knob of unsalted butter

1 tsp chipotle adobo, plus more to serve (optional)

400ml chicken stock

2 tbsp crème fraîche or sour cream

small bunch of coriander, chopped

Sit a cob on its end on a board. Cut the kernels from the cob with a small sharp knife in a downwards motion. Repeat for all the cobs.

Heat a heavy-based pan and slowly fry the onion and garlic with the tarragon and allspice in the olive oil. Add the sweetcorn kernels to the frying garlic and onion. Now add the butter and chipotle adobo, sweat for a few minutes until beginning to soften, add the stock and cook quickly until the sweetcorn is soft and the stock is reduced a little.

Ladle into bowls and serve with a spoonful of crème fraîche on top, sprinkled with the coriander. Sprinkle with a little more chipotle adobo too, if you like.

MORTARS AND PESTLES

I am a bit of a mortar and pestle addict. This kitchen gadget must be thousands of years old and is still the best. I am often frustrated abroad when I would love to buy a massive, local, stone mortar and pestle, but obviously cannot carry it around or put it on the plane. I am still bitter about the mortar and pestle I had to pass up on buying in the market in Oaxaca, South Mexico. It was enormous – wide and shallow – made from a beautiful coarse stone with splashes of bright colours. Perfect for making fresh, tasty guacamole. It must have weighed 50kg, well over the baggage allowance. I have, however, managed to acquire a goodly collection even with these restrictions. We have a couple I have had specially made: a large, wide, bowl-shaped mortar with a ball for a pestle, that is perfect for crushing beans or large pods, while a taller one is well-suited to making pastes.

The results you get from a mortar and pestle are really different from those you get using a blender. A blender cuts and whips, while a pestle presses and grinds, giving different-sized particles. These inconsistencies are what makes grinding by hand so beautiful. Pepper ground in a mortar and pestle has a lovely variety of textures, superior to that ground in a mill. Pounding releases different aromas in spices than those achieved by the cutting action of those little coffee grinders that many people use to grind spices.

It's great to have a few different mortars and pestles, as they are all good for different things. When making curry pastes I always reach for my tall ceramic mortar and pestle from Thailand, you can bash and grind and crush lots of different things at the same time and you won't end up with chillies and ginger all over your work surface. For grinding fennel seeds, I reach for my coarse composite green stone mortar and pestle; for pesto the marble set that is so like those I have seen in Liguria.

The main reason I love to use a mortar and pestle is that it is so satisfying. It can be slow – and it is harder work – but it is immensely rewarding.

A few weeks into the season – as soon as the spring vegetables which were babies start to look a bit more teenage and the first boxes of basil start to arrive – I make this delicious soup. You cook it for a long time, the flavours swap and smudge together into a beautiful, thick, rich vegetable mush, enlivened by proper pesto made with good basil.

LIGURIAN MINESTRA WITH PESTO

SERVES 6

2 small red onions, finely chopped

1 heart of celery, finely chopped

3 carrots, finely chopped

3 tbsp good olive oil, plus 100ml for the pesto

600g peas in the pod, podded weight (keep the pods)

600g broad beans in the pod, podded weight

2 bunches of asparagus, chopped the size of peas

150g large waxy potatoes, peeled and very thinly sliced (2mm)

sea salt

1 garlic clove, green sprout removed

2 large bunches of basil, preferably the small-leaf Ligurian variety

1 tsp pine nuts

1 tbsp finely grated parmesan

In a large, heavy-based pan, slowly fry the onions, celery, and carrots in the 3 tbsp oil for about 30 minutes, until really soft and sweet. This initial process is really important as it provides depth of flavour for your soup. Once the base is completely cooked, add the peas, broad beans, asparagus and potatoes, stir and continue to fry very gently for 45 minutes. Add a splash of water if it starts to catch on the base of the pan.

Bring a small pan of salted water to a boil, add the pea pods, cook for five minutes then drain (keep the water). Blend the pods with a little of their blanching water until almost smooth, then push the mixture though a sieve, extracting a small amount of very tasty green paste.

When all of the vegetables are almost soft, add some of the pea water to the pan – almost to the level of the top of the vegetables – and continue to cook until everything is completely soft and a beautiful khaki colour. Add the pea pod purée and set aside, off the heat, while you make the pesto.

In a mortar and pestle, crush the garlic clove with a pinch of coarse salt until completely smooth, then add the basil leaves and crush until smooth, then pour in the 100ml olive oil, pine nuts and parmesan.

Taste the soup, it should be rich, thick and tasty, the vegetables completely cooked and the potato broken down. Serve a bowl of the soup with a spoon of the pesto poured over. A hunk of parmesan, pecorino or salted ricotta and a bottle of olive oil will be welcome additions to the table.

These three toasts are one of the many summer combinations we make. The raw clams may seem a little left field, but they are excellent and don't feel weird at all when you eat them. If you can't find razor clams, a bit of fresh bass chopped up would work too, or a can of really good bonito.

THREE LITTLE TOASTS FOR SUMMER: RAZOR CLAMS, SAMPHIRE AND TOMATOES

SERVES 4

4 live razor clams

sea salt

good olive oil

handful of samphire, picked through, little black bits removed

4 large slices of coarse sourdough bread

1 garlic clove, halved

4 large ripe, sweet, tomatoes (I use the Marinda variety)

To prepare the razor clams, rinse them well in cold water then prise them open with your hands. Inside the clam is a white firm tube among the more slimy parts, pull this bit out and finely chop it. Put these tiny slices of clam into a bowl and season with a little salt (they will already be slightly salty) and douse in olive oil.

Briefly boil the samphire and dress with a little olive oil.

Heat a chargrill pan and toast the bread until dark and crunchy on both sides, then cut each piece into three. Scrape the clove of garlic over the top of four of them, then squash the tomatoes into the toast and pour over a little olive oil. Season with salt.

Put the chopped razor clams on four other toasts and the samphire on to the remaining four.

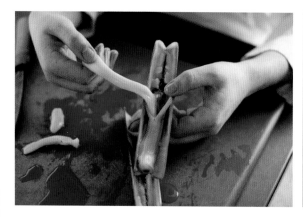

Diver scallops are much better than dredged, both in terms of taste and of environmental impact. This thoran is also very good without scallops, or with a bit of crab stirred through the peas.

PEA THORAN WITH SCALLOPS

SERVES 4

12 medium scallops, shelled

sea salt

olive oil

1 tsp brown mustard seeds

handful of fresh curry leaves, picked from stems

3 large mild dried chillies

500g small fresh peas in the pod, podded weight

½ coconut, peeled and finely grated (or 2 tbsp dried shredded coconut)

1 lemon

Heat a medium frying pan over a medium heat, season the scallops with salt and a little olive oil. When the pan is searingly hot, place the scallops into it. Leave them for around 90 seconds until nicely brown, then turn them over, reduce the heat and add the mustard seeds, then the curry leaves and chillies, followed by the peas.

Cook for another three minutes or so until the peas are just cooked, stirring through the coconut, then finish with a squeeze of lemon and a little more salt if needed. Serve with White or Brown Chapati (see page 183).

Saag aloo. Saag in India means any kind of greens. When I have visited markets in India, or in Indian parts of London, I'm always asking what the greens are called. They have spinach, fenugreek leaves, wild fennel, amaranth, all manner of different leaves, all of which are called saag. I use whatever I have around. It's easy to buy fenugreek leaves in Indian or Greek shops.

RAJASTHANI GREENS AND POTATOES

SERVES 4

150g large waxy potatoes, Cyprus or Roseval, peeled and cut into large cubes

sea salt

1 tsp cumin seeds

3 tbsp flavourless oil (I use mild olive oil)

¼ tsp turmeric

$^1/_8$ tsp fenugreek seeds

1 scant tsp ground coriander seeds

2 small, sweet red onions, finely chopped

3 garlic cloves, green sprouts removed, finely sliced

2.5cm fresh root ginger, peeled and coarsely grated

200g spinach or other greens, washed and shredded

2 ripe tomatoes, quartered

2 bunches of fenugreek leaves

3 tbsp yogurt

leaves from 1 small bunch of coriander

Boil the potatoes in a pan of well-salted, already boiling water until soft.

In a large, heavy-based pan over a medium-high heat, crackle the cumin in the oil, then add the other spices, followed quickly by the onions, garlic and ginger.

Reduce the heat and let the aromatics fry for about 15 minutes until completely soft and sweet. Add the shredded greens, tomatoes and fenugreek leaves and increase the heat. When the leaves have wilted, add the potatoes and a couple of spoonfuls of yogurt. Cook for a further 10 minutes, don't worry if the green starts to brown, it will still be delicious, perhaps more so. Stir in the coriander and serve.

This is a pretty salad I serve when we have a lot of flowers in the garden and the tomatoes are particularly good. Freekeh is an unusual Lebanese wheat with which I am obsessed. It's picked while still underripe and set on fire to remove the husk, which smokes and toasts the grain.

TOMATO SALAD WITH FLOWERS, ZA'ATAR AND FREEKEH

SERVES 4

50g freekeh or farro

sea salt

olive oil

1 tbsp pomegranate molasses

6 tomatoes of great flavour, colour and ripeness

1 scant tsp za'atar

a few edible flowers, I usually have violas, rocket flowers, or borage to hand in the summer

Wash the freekeh or farro and boil it gently in unseasoned water for up to an hour, or just 20 minutes, depending on your freekeh (some are broken grains, others whole). It should be soft but still slightly chewy. Drain, then season with salt and dress with olive oil.

In a little bowl, whisk the pomegranate molasses with 3 tbsp olive oil to make an emulsified dressing.

Slice the tomatoes thinly, in little wedges or round slices, a way that looks pretty and is sensitive to their natural shape. Toss with salt and a little olive oil. Lay the tomatoes on a plate, scatter with the freekeh, za'atar and edible flowers. Finish the plate by drizzling with the pomegranate molasses mixture.

The best potatoes for gnocchi are gnarly old big floury ones; they just taste better and make soft, floury gnocchi. Waxy potatoes make waxy gnocchi. In the summer I make this light, fast tomato sauce. In the winter I use jarred tomatoes and cook it really slowly to an intense, sweetly acidic concoction.

POTATO GNOCCHI AND TOMATO SAUCE

SERVES 4

For the gnocchi

6 large floury potatoes

1 egg yolk

2 handfuls of plain flour, plus more to dust

fine salt

coarse semolina, to dust (optional)

salted ricotta, parmesan, or aged pecorino, to serve

For the tomato sauce

20 ripe, soft plum tomatoes

4 garlic cloves, green sprouts removed, thinly sliced

olive oil

1 small hot dried chilli, crumbled

sea salt

very large handful of basil

Preheat the oven to 180°C/350°F/gas mark 4. Bake the potatoes for 45 minutes to one hour, until soft to a knife.

Meanwhile, make the tomato sauce. Boil a large pan of water, slit the skin of the tomatoes and drop them into the water for 10 seconds or until the skin comes easily from the flesh. Remove from the water and rinse. Peel, squeeze and finely chop, discarding the core. Heat a wide shallow pan, fry the garlic in a good glug of olive oil until it starts to stick together and brown slightly, then add the chilli followed by the tomatoes. Season well with salt and increase the heat until everything bubbles nicely. Reduce the heat while you make the gnocchi.

Boil a large pan of well-salted water. Cut the potatoes in half and scoop out the insides. Push the potato through a coarse sieve or ricer. Turn this on to a work surface. Add the egg yolk and flour with a good pinch of fine salt. Bring together to form a soft dough, break a bit off and drop it into the boiling water. If it dissolves, add more flour until a little dumpling more or less holds its form. Try to work the dough as little as possible and add as little flour as you need to bring the dough together.

Roll the dough into a long sausage around 3cm in diameter, dusting with flour or semolina. Cut it into shapes as long as they are wide, don't worry if they are not uniform. Make a dimple in each with your finger, using a slight rolling motion; this helps hold the sauce. Dust with flour, then pop them into the water.

Add the basil to the sauce then, when the gnocchi have risen to the surface and simmered for a couple of minutes, remove them to the sauce. Stir a little and serve with parmesan, aged pecorino, or, ideally, salted ricotta.

Richard Olney's *Simple French Cooking* made me interested in vegetable ragoûts. He wrote a beautiful piece about how to cook them in heavy, cast-iron pans, adding different vegetables according to cooking time and how they are cut. He explained about leaving the lid only half-covered if the vegetables give off too much liquid, adding a splash of water or wine if they are dry. Look after your ragoût while its cooking but don't mollycoddle it. Trust your instincts. Often dishes benefit from a little ignoring...

RAGOÛT DE LÉGUMES SUMMER

SERVES 6

3 garlic cloves, green sprouts removed, thinly sliced

1 small red onion, thinly sliced

2 tbsp olive oil

1 large aubergine (I get big round ones from the south of Italy), cut into large dice

1 large red pepper (not a Dutch one, they're generally tasteless), halved, deseeded and cut into strips

3 small firm courgettes, cut into wedges

handful of young and very fresh broad beans left in the pods, cut diagonally into 1cm pieces

3 plum tomatoes, in 1cm slices

150g fresh peas in the pod, podded weight

sea salt

freshly ground black pepper

leaves from 1 small bunch of basil

In a medium, heavy-based, preferably cast-iron pot, slowly fry the garlic and onion in olive oil. After a few minutes, add the aubergine and pepper, increase the heat a little and stir occasionally until they are starting to soften. Add the courgettes and broad beans, reduce the heat and cover with the lid.

After about 15 minutes, add the tomatoes and peas. Continue to cook, with the lid on or off depending on how liquid the mixture is. When everything is soft and tasty, check the seasoning and add the basil leaves. Eat warm or at room temperature, with toast, salad or nothing. Rosé would be nice.

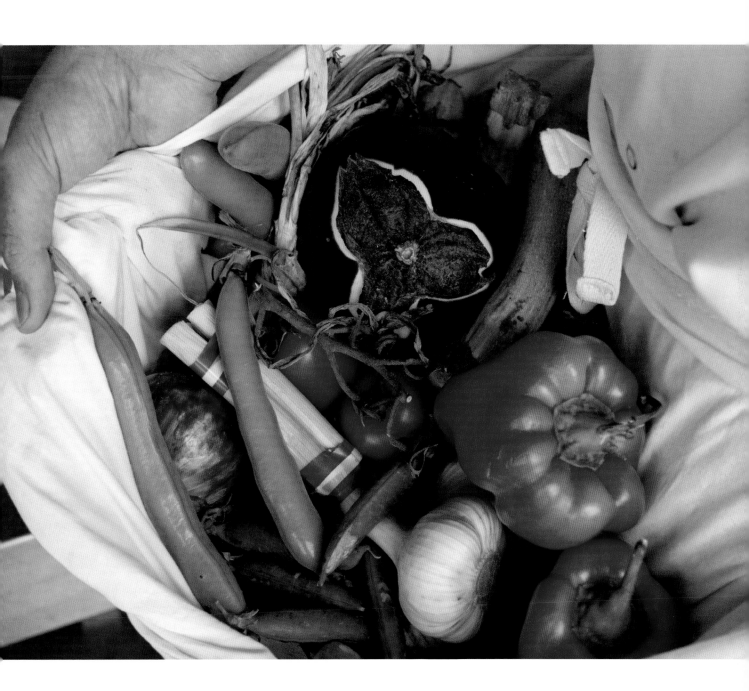

I always use frozen octopus as fresh can be such a disaster. Sometimes they never go soft, though when they do they taste great. People have lots of tricks for getting an octopus to become tender: hitting it with a hammer; dipping it in and out of boiling water; freezing and defrosting it... I find it easier to buy a good frozen specimen. I nicked this recipe from my great friend Tommi Miers who runs a group of Mexican fast food restaurants. Sometimes she comes to cook Mexican dinners with us at Dock Kitchen.

MEXICAN OCTOPUS AND PORK CRACKLING WITH TOMATO SALSA

SERVES ABOUT 6

1 frozen Spanish octopus (about 1kg)

sunflower oil, to deep-fry

200ml whole milk

150g fine semolina

100g pack of pork scratchings

For the salsa

2-3 large, ripe tomatoes

2 spring onions

2 fresh jalapeño chillies (or any mild green chilli)

bunch of coriander

sea salt

juice of 2 limes

Defrost the octopus in a sink and wash well (sometimes the suckers hold little bits of sand). Where all the legs meet, just below the eyes, is the beak, a hard black part; remove this with a small sharp knife. Discard the mush inside the head. Place the cleaned octopus in a large pan of cold water and bring it to a boil over a medium heat. Reduce the heat and cook for around an hour, until it is tender. Remove from the pan and discard the liquid. Cut the legs into 1cm slices and the head into thin rings.

Heat a deep-fat fryer or large pan with the sunflower oil to 180°C (350°F).

Meanwhile, chop the tomatoes roughly. Finely chop the spring onions and chillies together and roughly chop the coriander. Mix all these chopped ingredients together, add a little salt, then squeeze over and stir in the lime. Taste the salsa, it should be hot and strong.

Dip the slices of octopus into the milk, then dust them in the semolina. Deep-fry until crisp, then drain on kitchen paper. Crush the pork scratchings into dust in a mortar and pestle, then sprinkle over the octopus. Serve with the salsa on top.

This is a recipe that one of our chefs, Alex, picked up in Morocco. As is sometimes the case with finding dishes in exotic places, the original wasn't that good. The cuttlefish was chewy, the onion undercooked and the whole thing a bit dry... But the spicing was fascinating, the dried oregano adding a classic Mediterranean taste to a coastal Moroccan dish, so it got noted down and transported to Dock Kitchen where we worked on it together.

CUTTLEFISH TAGINE

SERVES 6

For the tagine

1 red onion, roughly chopped

good glug of olive oil

1 head of new garlic, sliced thinly

sea salt

3kg cuttlefish, cleaned and cut into thin strips

5 fresh tomatoes, cut up not too small

8 waxy (I use Roseval) potatoes, cut into thin wedges

bunch of coriander, roughly chopped

about 20 large green olives

For the spice mix

5 tsp coriander seeds, toasted and ground

2 tsp cumin seeds, toasted and ground

4 tsp allspice berries, ground

2 tsp cayenne

2 tsp mild paprika

1 whole nutmeg, grated

½ tsp ground cinnamon

½ tsp caraway seeds

¼ tsp anise seeds

1 tsp fennel seeds

4 pinches of dried oregano

pinch of saffron

10 cardamom pods, bashed about

5 pinches of dried rose petals

Mix together all the ingredients for the spice mix. In a large, heavy-based pan, cook the onion in the oil. Add the garlic and a big pinch of salt and cook for about 10 minutes, until soft. Add about half the spice mix and cook gently for a few minutes.

Increase the heat to medium, add the cuttlefish and fry for about 10 minutes. Add the tomatoes and potatoes and check the spice, adding more to taste. Half-cover with a lid and cook at a simmer for about 20 minutes, or until both the cuttlefish and the potatoes are cooked.

When the cuttlefish is cooked, add half the coriander and cook for a further five minutes. Add the olives right at the end and sprinkle a bit more coriander on when you are ready to eat, less because it's pretty than because it's good to have the taste of cooked and raw coriander on a rich dish like this.

Turbot can be so expensive it is crazy. You could use brill or halibut for this recipe as well. This sauce always reminds me of Skye Gyngell at Petersham Nurseries. Skye is a beautiful cook. We used to make a version of it often when I worked there, she called it Green Goddess sauce, the name has something or other to do with Louis XIII.

POACHED TURBOT GREEN GODDESS WITH SWISS CHARD AND SAMPHIRE SERVES 6

sea salt

1kg Swiss chard with large juicy white stalks, leaves stripped from stalks, stalks chopped into thin strips

500g samphire, picked, little black bits removed

2 egg yolks

2 anchovy fillets

½ tsp Dijon mustard

250ml olive oil, plus more to serve

handful of mixed dill, tarragon, chervil and parsley

4 tbsp crème fraîche

1 x 3kg turbot, cut into 6 'tranches' (head removed, split along backbone and each half cut into 3 steaks on the bone)

For the court bouillon

½ bottle crisp white wine

2 bay leaves

1 tsp black peppercorns

1 tsp fennel seeds

a few parsley stalks

piece of lemon zest

Bring a large pan of well-salted water to a boil and boil the chard stalks until soft, followed by the leaves and the samphire. Drain well and spread on a large plate to cool.

In a blender or food processor, whizz the egg yolks, anchovies, mustard and a little salt. Very slowly add the olive oil, allowing the emulsion to thicken before adding some more. If you are a confident mayonnaise-maker you can go quite fast, watching the emulsion carefully you can see when to pause and allow the oil to incorporate properly. If not, drip, drip, drip is the way to go. When you have added all the oil, add the herbs and blend until pale green. Stir in the crème fraîche and set aside.

Put all the ingredients for the court bouillon with a handful of salt into a wide pan that will fit all your pieces of turbot and top up with enough water to cover the fish. Bring to a boil then add the turbot, reduce the heat right down and cook for five minutes on a very gentle simmer. Now turn the pan off and leave for a further five minutes.

Serve the turbot with the chard and samphire, warm or at room temperature, dressed in a little olive oil, with the green goddess sauce on top.

Freekeh is one of my favourite ingredients. I first came across it on a trip to Lebanon. It's a delicious and versatile ingredient. I import it, but you can find it in Lebanese shops (and Selfridges). Apparently, this unique treatment of wheat was discovered by accident thousands of years ago when, during a year of drought, an unripe field of wheat caught fire. After the fire the owners couldn't afford to waste the grain, so picked through the ashy fields. They must have been delighted with the result.

MACKEREL WITH FREEKEH, AUBERGINES AND TAHINI SAUCE

SERVES 4

400g freekeh
2 large aubergines
olive oil
sea salt
freshly ground black pepper
150g small fresh peas in the pod, podded weight
150g spinach leaves
4 lovely and fresh large mackerel
1 garlic clove, green sprout removed
2 tbsp tahini
2 lemons, plus lemon wedges to serve
1 tsp Lebanese Seven Spice (see page 182), or a cinnamon stick and a few crushed allspice berries
leaves from 1 small bunch of parsley, chopped
sumac, to serve (optional)

Wash the freekeh well, then boil it until the grain is soft but a little al dente. This might take as much as an hour or just 20 minutes depending on your freekeh (some are broken grains, others whole).

Preheat the oven to 220°C/425°F/gas mark 7 (if you have a fancy oven, put the grill on as well as the oven). Cut the aubergines into cubes a couple of centimetres wide and toss in olive oil, salt and pepper. Roast in the oven until completely soft and nicely browned (no one likes a half-cooked aubergine).

Blanch the peas in well-salted water for a couple of minutes, then drain. Blanch the spinach very briefly just until wilted, then drain and spead out on a plate to cool.

Put the mackerel into a roasting tray, season with salt and drizzle with olive oil. Roast in the hot oven (and grill, if you can) for about 10 minutes, until the flesh pulls easily from the bone.

Meanwhile, make the tahini sauce: crush the garlic with a little salt, add the tahini and a spoonful of water, followed by the lemon juice. The mixture will immediately turn very thick, so let it down with water and a spoonful or two of olive oil.

Drain the freekeh and mix it with the seven spice, roasted aubergine, peas, spinach and chopped parsley. Serve next to a grilled mackerel with tahini sauce all splodged on and the whole thing sprinkled with sumac (if you have some) and some lemon wedges.

MIDDLE EASTERN INGREDIENTS

The Middle East is a big place and there are several sophisticated and fascinating food cultures within it. My favourite of those I have visited is Lebanon. Lebanese cooking is right up my street. Ingredients led – you can see the excitement in the market when the first loquats arrive, or the small scrum to buy the limited number of wild thistles or fresh za'atar – fresh, tasty and zingy. There are loads of fantastic ingredients that you can get quite easily over here; we sell a few of them at Dock Kitchen.

Pomegranate molasses is one of my favourites. Good-quality bottles have no ingredient other than pomegranate juice which has been boiled down to a thick, black, intense, sweet-and-sour syrup. We also use a lot of distilled flower waters, rose and orange blossom are the most common, though I have also come across lemon blossom and jasmine. Rose and orange blossom waters are distilled from the flowers, they should smell beautiful and fragrant but not confected. I think the cheaper flower waters are often chemically enhanced.

Sumac is the ground berry of a beautiful wild bush. It is red in colour (though shouldn't be too brightly red) and wonderfully zingy. I often use it in salads (particularly in a fattoush of bread, tomato, herbs and cheese) instead of lemon or vinegar.

Za'atar is a slightly confusing word. It is the name applied to a group of herbs that grow wild on Mount Lebanon. As far as I can tell (I went picking them on the mountain), they are a mixture of types of oregano, savory/thyme and sage. The herbs can be used fresh, but are usually dried and crushed into a powder, then mixed with sumac and sesame seeds, sometimes a little toasted crushed cumin.

Freekeh is my absolute favourite. We have loads of it sent over by a friend of mine from the south of Lebanon. It's a kind of wheat, a little like the Italian farro. Except it is picked while still underripe and green, then set on fire. The husk burns off and toasts and smokes the grain, leaving a delicious green, smoky grain, quite unlike any other I have tasted. It's a staple in my home and restaurant.

AUBERGINES This is a plate both simple and delicious. We don't always put fenugreek in the labne, but it can add a lovely, savoury, slightly musty taste that is most welcome with the bitter, earthy aubergines.

SARDINES Chermoula can be used with lots of different fish. Vary it as you like: I don't always use saffron, but herbs and acidity are important. Harissa is useful to have in the fridge. It brightens up the dullest lunch.

ROAST AUBERGINES AND LABNE

SERVES 4

400ml yogurt

¼ tsp fenugreek seeds, ground

sea salt

2 large aubergines

olive oil

1 small hot dried chilli, crumbled

½ cinnamon stick, ground

½ tsp coriander seeds, coarsely crushed

Mix the yogurt with the ground fenugreek and season to taste. Wrap in a clean cloth (a tea towel, apron, or muslin) and place in a sieve or colander over a bowl, either in the fridge or just somewhere cool. Leave for about 12 hours.

Preheat the oven to 200°C/400°F/gas mark 6. Slice the aubergines into thick slices, drizzle with olive oil and sprinkle with salt, chilli, cinnamon and coriander. Roast in the hot oven until the slices are well-browned and completely soft. Unwrap the labne, spread it out on a plate and serve the aubergines on top.

SARDINES IN CHERMOULA WITH HARISSA

SERVES 4

12 sardines, butterflied

a few spoons of harissa

For the chermoula

½ bunch of parsley

½ bunch of coriander

2 garlic cloves, green sprouts removed

½ tsp paprika

a few threads of saffron

1 scant tsp lightly toasted ground cumin

glug of olive oil

1 thumb of fresh root ginger, peeled and roughly chopped

1 ripe tomato, quartered

juice of 1 lemon

pinch of salt

Preheat the grill to its highest setting. Blend all the ingredients for the chermoula together in a food processor, then rub the mixture on to the sardines. Lay them flat in a tray, skin side up, then grill them under the hot grill for three to four minutes.

Eat them with a little harissa. These sardines are also delicious in a sandwich. In the brilliant Moroccan stall near Dock Kitchen they put a few chips in the bread roll too. It's delicious.

I love this delicious yogurt marinade for chicken. It takes a second to make and is brilliant with Lemon Pickle (see page 186). Also, of course, good with a shop-bought pickle, just not quite as good. Keralan Cauliflower and Potatoes (see page 85) would be nice with it. Choose a good chicken; I like a scrawny, long-legged specimen that looks as though it has lived a good life.

SPICED CHICKEN WITH LEMON PICKLE AND FLATBREAD

SERVES 6

1 tsp cumin seeds

1 tbsp coriander seeds

½ tsp turmeric

2 fresh red chillies

½ bunch of coriander, finely chopped

150g yogurt

1 chicken, off the bone (a friendly butcher will do it for you)

Preheat the oven to 220°C/425°F/gas mark 7.

Place the cumin seeds in a dry frying pan over a medium heat and toast them, stirring, until they smell aromatic. Tip them into a mortar with the coriander and turmeric and grind them together. Then add the fresh chillies and grind them, as well, into a fine paste. Now stir in the coriander and grind a little more, then stir in the yogurt.

Rub this yogurt mixture on the chicken. Cook the chicken in the oven or on a barbecue for about 20 minutes until, when you cut into the thickest part, it is opaque and white, not translucent and pink. It's really easy to serve.

If you barbecue the chicken you can cook the flatbread on the barbecue too, which people always find amazing. Serve with Lemon Pickle (see page 186) and Grilled Yeasted Flatbread (see page 185).

THE RIGHT TOOLS

What you cook with makes a massive difference to how your food ends up. I'm not just talking about good-quality heavy-based pans, though they are important. Heavy pans distribute heat evenly, rather than in little hot spots over the points of heat, meaning that whatever is in the pan can cook evenly and gently over a low heat. Also, when very hot, they retain heat to keep intensity when you add something cool to the pan. Good steel or copper pans last for many years and are worth every penny.

However, sometimes a good-quality stainless steel pan won't do as well as a rougher, more authentic vessel: a cast-iron cauldron, a terracotta cazuela, a thick dosa pan or a coarse pottery tagine. These unusual receptacles not only conjure up images of the places from which they come, but also seem to make the food more authentic too. Sometimes, when I am finding the true taste of a dish I have had somewhere else difficult to recreate, I realise it's because I'm using the wrong pan; even using a ceramic baking tray instead of a metal one can make a significant difference.

At the restaurant we have a tandoor oven. It is really just a big clay pot with a charcoal fire at the bottom. Difficult to control – and easy to burn yourself – you may wonder why we bother. Because the tandoor cooks like nothing else. It has a hot, smoky environment, both from the incredibly hot, thick walls of the oven and also from the immense heat produced by the charcoal. Basically it both bakes and barbecues. We cook flatbreads on its side and they are ready in 90 seconds.

Not many people will be lucky enough to have a tandoor oven at home (though buying one is cheaper and easier than a wood oven or even a fancy barbecue), but lots have a barbecue. And shouldn't be afraid to use it. Barbecuing is about much more than burnt sausages. You can cook more exciting things if you try. The most important thing is being able to regulate the temperature. Barbecues where you can lift the racks away from the coals are the best as, when the fire is hot, you can still grill gently. Grilling meat or fish slowly over glowing red-white coals gives a beautiful flavour.

A truly simple recipe, this really shows the incredibly umami qualities of fish sauce in bringing out every bit of hidden flavour from a potentially bland, farmed quail. It can be tricky to bone a quail, so ask your butcher to do it if you're not very confident about it.

THAI GRILLED QUAIL

SERVES 4

4 quails, off the bone

sea salt

1 tsp olive oil

4 very small, hot red chillies

4 tbsp fish sauce

Heat a heavy cast-iron grill pan or prepare your barbecue to a well rounded, white heat. Season the quails with salt and rub in a little olive oil, then place them skin side down on the grill.

Quickly chop the chillies and mix into the fish sauce in a little bowl. Once the quail skin is well browned, turn them over and cook for a few more seconds. Serve rare, dipping them into the hot fish sauce. This dish probably needs a cold beer with it.

I first cooked this recipe from a Richard Olney cookbook when I was working at Petersham. Richard Olney was a brilliant American food writer. I can't remember how close to the original this is, but it is surely a brilliant, simple, summery dish. It's unusual to eat cooked cucumbers (though there is a delicious Sri Lankan cucumber curry I make sometimes). This is a recipe for farmed rabbit; the stronger gamey taste of a wild one would not sit well with the delicately flavoured ingredients.

RABBIT WITH CUCUMBERS, TOMATOES, ROSÉ AND BASIL

SERVES 4

1 rabbit, jointed (front legs, back legs and saddle cut into 2)

sea salt

freshly ground black pepper

couple of glugs of olive oil

large pinch of saffron

1 small sweet red onion, very thinly sliced

3 garlic cloves, green sprouts removed, cut into little chips

½ bottle of Provençal rosé wine

4 small cucumbers, cut into little wedges

350g tomatoes (the best you can find, cherry, bull's heart, whatever is tastiest) cut the size of the cucumbers

big handful of basil

Preheat the oven to 180°C/350°F/gas mark 4. Put the rabbit joints in a deep roasting tray and season with salt and pepper, olive oil, saffron, onion and garlic. Pour in the wine and seal with foil, then bake for an hour; the rabbit should be tender but not browned.

Remove the tray from the oven and increase the oven temperature to 220°C/425°F/gas mark 7. Add the cucumbers and tomatoes and drizzle with a little olive oil. Return the tray to the oven, uncovered, and roast until nicely browned and the tomatoes and cucumbers are cooked. Throw in the basil and serve with a glass of rosé and a hunk of good bread.

This recipe is about chillies, beautiful dried, smoked chillies from Mexico. You can buy all sorts of great Mexican things at coolchile.co.uk. Spanish shops sell similar, unsmoked versions of Mexican peppers: guindillas and ñoras. Once you have found the peppers, choose those which look most exciting and chuck them in the pan with the pork.

MEXICAN PORK SHOULDER

SERVES 8–10

1 pork shoulder, off the bone (about 2kg)

6 ancho chillies

3 pasilla de Oaxaca

10 bay leaves

6 tomatoes

250ml vinegar (a delicate red wine vinegar would be perfect)

1 head of garlic, broken into cloves

For the salsa

3 ripe tomatoes

small bunch of coriander

1 small sweet red onion, very finely chopped

sea salt

2 limes

1 large green chilli, finely chopped

Preheat the oven to 180°C/350°F/gas mark 4. Put the pork shoulder, chillies, bay, tomatoes, vinegar and garlic into a wide pan or baking tray. Top up with water to cover about two-thirds of the way up the joint. Cover with foil and bake for three hours.

Remove the foil from the meat and increase the oven temperature to 220°C/425°F/gas mark 7. Roast until the meat is a deep brown colour.

For the salsa, chop the tomatoes roughly and the coriander fine, mix with the onion and season well with salt and lime juice, adding the chilli to taste. Tear the meat up a little and serve a pile of it with a bit of the sour, hot juice. Top with the salsa.

AUTUMN

I had a soup a little like at this at the house of my friend, the photographer Jason Lowe. I recreated it a year or so later, so it may or may not be similar to the original... I often serve it with melon, or cherries in the summer, some blended in, some on the top. It's a pretty magical soup. You are going slowly to build the flavours by adding different things to the blender and tasting as you go. It's complex in taste: gentle acidity balances rich nuts, while the perfume of rose water competes with garlic and herbs.

IRANIAN PISTACHIO, CUCUMBER AND GRAPES SOUP

SERVES 6

75g blanched almonds

75g fresh green pistachios or 3 tbsp unsweetened pistachio purée

1 garlic clove, green sprout removed

1 cucumber, roughly chopped

100g sweet red grapes

leaves from 1 small bunch of mint

a few sprigs of dill

1 tbsp rose water

juice of 1 lemon

sea salt

a few strands of saffron, to serve

Start with the almonds, pistachios and garlic, blending until completely fine in a food processor or blender. Now blend a little more, adding a few spoonfuls of water. Once the mixture starts to smell of marzipan you can start to add the other ingredients.

Tip in the cucumber and half the grapes, most of the mint leaves and dill. Add a little rose water – be careful as bottles can vary in strength – a squeeze of lemon and enough water to make a thin soup.

Season with salt and taste, you should be able to detect all the ingredients individually, but none too strongly. Add more of anything you think you want to taste a little more; trust your instincts. Serve with ice cubes if it is hot, the remaining grapes, sliced, the remaining herbs, and the strands of saffron.

THE INFLUENCE OF ITALY

At the moment I don't cook that much Italian food, but its influence pervades most of the dishes I make. The Italians know how to eat. I love the form of an Italian meal. It begins with antipasti, which could be cooked vegetables, cured ham, cheese, things that are nice with an aperitivo. Then follows a starchy primi of pasta, soup or rice, then a simple meat or fish main course with sides of vegetables with olive oil, followed by cheese, then dessert. It's a form I often imitate even when cooking from a culture that doesn't usually have this kind of meal. I love eating the carbohydrate before the protein and starting with delicious little things to share.

Italians never put too many ingredients on the plate. This simple, restrained food is not, as many assume, always peasant cooking. Much of it is – and we can learn a lot from the rural Italian *cucina povera*, particularly from the south – but much of the Italian food we love is the smart food of the grand cities of Italy. Why else are many of the great dishes named after the cities they were invented in: osso bucco Milanese; bistecca Fiorentina; ragu de Bologna; focaccia di Genovese... Italian food is a kind of cooking minimalism. It has evolved over generations of sophisticated cooks paring down what they do. And we can all learn from this simple, subtle approach.

"Al contadino non far sapere quanto è buono il formaggio con le pere"
Do not tell the peasant how good the cheese tastes with the pear

Italian cooks are very good at seasoning. I don't just mean salt. They use anchovies, porcini mushrooms, chilli, fennel seeds, herbs, flecks of tomato and black pepper with purpose and insight, adding depth, interest and vibrancy to dishes in ways that are absent from many other food cultures. Because of this clever use of seasonings, Italian food is immensely satisfying. This is something we can carry over into all our cooking; it's good to taste everything like an Italian mama. Make sure that your cooking is punchy when it should be, delicate when you want it to be and always restrained, like a grand Italian nonna in Bologna.

You could add a few pieces of pancetta to this soup to great effect. You can use fresh porcini instead of dried if you want, but probably not a different kind of mushroom.

BARLEY AND PORCINI SOUP

20g good-quality dried porcini

1 red onion, roughly chopped

1 celery heart, roughly chopped

olive oil

leaves from 2 sprigs of thyme

4 bay leaves

2 tomatoes, roughly chopped

200g pearl barley

sea salt

freshly ground black pepper

best olive oil, to serve

Soak the dried mushrooms in 200ml of boiling water.

Fry the onion and celery in a generous amount of olive oil until it is really deep in flavour and slightly brown; this is the base, the soffritto, and forms the basis of all the flavour so it's important to get it tasting great. It should take about 25 minutes to get really good.

Drain the porcini (but keep the liquid) and roughly chop them. Add to the soffritto with the thyme, bay and tomatoes and cook for another few minutes. Add the barley and the porcini water, cover with more water and cook gently for about an hour. Season well with salt and pepper and serve, thick, liberally topped with your best olive oil.

In the absence of fresh borlotti beans you could use good-quality dried beans, soaked overnight. It's important that the beef is dry-aged so it has good flavour and texture; chop it with a knife, don't try to mince it.

THREE LITTLE TOASTS FOR AUTUMN: BEEF, BORLOTTI BEANS AND CHARD

SERVES 4

100g aged beef (topside or silverside, or any other lean, cheap cut)

good olive oil

sea salt

150g fresh borlotti beans (podded weight)

1 tomato

3 garlic cloves, 2 left whole, the other with the green sprout removed and finely sliced

1 tbsp red wine vinegar

150g Swiss chard

½ tsp fennel seeds, coarsely crushed

sea salt

freshly ground black pepper

4 large slices of coarse sourdough bread

Using a large, sharp knife, finely chop the beef until it is almost completely smooth, then mix with a little olive oil and some salt.

In a small saucepan with a lid, place the borlotti beans, the tomato and one of the whole garlic cloves. Cover with water, then the lid and cook gently for around an hour until the beans are soft. Drain most of the remaining water, season with salt, a splash of red wine vinegar and a glug of olive oil.

Boil a medium pan of water. Chop the chard stalks quite small and the leaves bigger. Season the water well then boil the chard stalks. After a few minutes, once they are soft, add the leaves and cook for another couple of minutes. Drain the chard and let it sit in a colander.

Return the empty pan to the heat and add a good glug of olive oil, the sliced garlic and fennel seeds. Once the garlic starts to brown slightly and stick together, return the chard and season well. Braise the greens for a few minutes until completely soft and well flavoured.

Heat a cast-iron chargrill pan. Toast your bread until dark and crunchy. Rub the remaining halved garlic clove on the bread and cut each toast into three pieces. Spread each of the toppings – raw meat, warm beans, or room temperature chard – on four of the toasts. Pour over a little good olive oil and serve.

WILD FOOD

It's almost impossible to read a restaurant menu at the moment without seeing the word 'wild' at least a few times. Often it's practically meaningless. Wild rocket, for example, is just a variety: the thin spiky one, as opposed to the floppy-leaved domestic one. That's not to say it can't actually be wild, just that it rarely is. The same is true of asparagus. Wild asparagus is the very skinny kind (see right), it grows wild in England and much of Europe and North Africa. When ingredients are genuinely wild, they taste different. They've had a hard life, they haven't been planted in neat little rows, fed and watered regularly. They've self-seeded, grown in nooks and crannies and relied on the changeable weather for nourishment. This leads to strong, concentrated flavours.

At Dock Kitchen we are lucky enough to have a forager, Miles Irving, based in Kent (forager.org.uk). He finds all manner of wild plants, especially in late summer and autumn.

We have quite a few dishes at Dock Kitchen that rely on wild ingredients. Kibbeh (or kubbeh) is a word used to describe any of the Middle Eastern bulgar wheat dishes. We make a kibbeh with crushed wild oregano, rocket and fennel mixed into the bulgar wheat, finishing it with semi-crushed beautiful wild flowers. It's quite a classic Lebanese dish that was cooked for me by a friend on a trip to Beirut. She told me how it was made by workers in the fields, picking edible herbs and flowers as they worked and crushing them into the bulgar wheat to make a delicious, green, healthful paste. We also use mixed wild herbs and greens to flavour gnudi (naked or nude ravioli).

Wild mushrooms are one of the highlights of the wild food year. Often the simplest recipes are the best: ceps fried in garlic and oil on toast must be one of the best things to eat at any time of day, or the same mushrooms cooked in butter and mixed into tagliatelle with parsley. My favourite wild mushroom dish is based on a recipe I came across in a Kashmiri cookbook for morel and black cumin pilau. The mushrooms work perfectly with the earthy flavour of black cumin and the almost musty taste of exotic saffron.

Sea vegetables are also abundant in the summer and the most well-known of them is samphire. Samphire is a delicious salty vegetable with a slight asparagus taste. You can buy it easily at the fishmonger during warmer months. I often serve it as a side with fish, or occasionally meat. Sometimes I add a bit to a pan of clams, or use it raw as a salad with some cucumber next to a piece of cured fish.

Foraging some of the lesser-known plants requires real skill, however there are many wild things that taste great and are easy to buy or find. Mallow flowers, wild sweet peas, borage and rocket all grow rampantly and are easy to identify. Fruits such as blackcurrants, cherries and elderberries are easy to find even in cities, so we should all be heading to the hedgerows to get tasty free food. Every year masses of cherries go to waste all around the UK. The small sour fruits, almost inedible when raw, are usually left to the birds, but they are delicious when cooked and make a really lovely pot of jam, or a beautiful sour cherry pie.

opposite, clockwise from top left:
wild radicchio; monk's beard/agretti;
lovage; samphire; wild asparagus;
dandelion

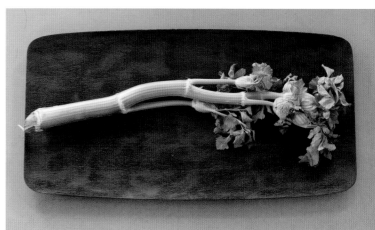

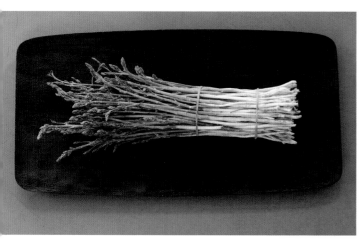

We serve this as a starter, though usually it would be a dish in a big thali, a south Indian rice and curry meal. It's nice to have a bit of lime pickle with a thoran. The heady, exotic taste of fresh curry leaves is really alluring, so do try and search them out; you'll find them in some supermarkets and lots of Indian grocers. If you can't get them, use fresh coriander rather than dried curry leaves.

BEETROOT THORAN

SERVES 4

250g beetroot with leaves (if possible), washed
2 tbsp vegetable oil
1 tsp mustard seeds
2 sprigs of fresh curry leaves, picked from stems
1 green chilli
1 small, sweet red onion, thinly sliced
salt
1 coconut, smashed, flesh peeled and grated
1 lemon

Coarsly grate the beetroot and finely slice the leaves. Heat a large frying pan over a high heat. Add the vegetable oil and then the mustard seeds. When the mustard seeds begin to crackle, add the curry leaves and green chilli, then the red onion and grated beetroot and leaves.

Season with salt and continue to stir-fry for about five minutes. Finish with the coconut and a squeeze of lemon. Serve with White or Brown Chapati (see page 183).

CHAAT MASALA Amchur is mango powder. You can buy it in Indian shops. This spice mix makes enough for a few meals and keeps well in a sealed jar. Don't worry if you don't have all the spices, just balance it nicely. CAULIFLOWER AND POTATOES The gobi aloo that Indian restaurant-goers in the UK know, but using classic southern Indian flavours of curry leaves and mustard seeds instead of lots of cumin, turmeric and chilli.

MANGO AND TOMATO CHAAT MASALA

SERVES 4

400g can of chickpeas

vegetable oil, to deep-fry

small bunch of fresh curry leaves, leaves picked from stems

1 mango, or ½ a pineapple

3 tomatoes

1 celery heart, finely chopped

salt

1 lemon

For the spice mix

2 tsp amchur

½ tsp coriander seeds

¼ tsp cumin seeds

¼ tsp dried chilli

½ tsp cardamom seeds

¼ tsp ground cinnamon

tiny pinch of asafoetida

Blend all the spices together in a mortar and pestle, pounding a little to bring them all together into a uniform masala (spice mix).

Drain, rinse and dry the chickpeas. Heat a medium pan with about 2.5cm of vegetable oil. When hot (about 160°C/325°F) add the chickpeas and fry for about three minutes until crispy, add the curry leaves and fry for a few more seconds. Remove from the oil, using a slotted spoon, and place on to a piece of kitchen paper.

Cut the mango flesh from the stone and peel off the skin. Cut the mango into small dice, don't worry if it mushes up a bit (or cut the pineapple into small dice, if using). Dice the tomatoes and celery heart small as well, then mix with the mango, fried chickpeas and curry leaves. Season well with salt then liberally sprinkle with the spice mix. Taste, adding lemon and more spice if necessary.

KERALAN CAULIFLOWER AND POTATOES

SERVES 4

200g potatoes

salt

2 tbsp vegetable oil

½ tsp mustard seeds

3 large mild dried chillies

handful of fresh curry leaves, picked from stems

1 red onion, finely chopped

2.5cm piece fresh root ginger, finely chopped

freshly ground black pepper

1 tsp ground coriander

1 small cauliflower, broken into florets

1 large ripe tomato, torn apart

Peel the potatoes, cut them into 5cm pieces and set them to boil in well-salted water.

Heat a wide pan over a high heat, pour in the oil and add the mustard seeds. When they crackle, add the dried chillies and curry leaves. When they start to splutter, add the onion and ginger and season well. Reduce the heat and add the coriander. Cook gently for 15 minutes, until the onion is really soft. Add the cauliflower, tomato and a splash of water, cover and cook for 10 minutes. Add the potatoes and cook for a few more minutes. Eat as a side dish, or on its own with White or Brown Chapati (see page 183).

It's lovely to cook a selection of small plates as a starter or as the whole meal, this one contains some of my favourite dishes. When AA Gill reviewed Dock Kitchen he said the clams tasted as though they had been cooked in Venus's bath water, which I think was a compliment; it was a five star review after all. The chicken livers dish is one of our most popular, a wonderful combination of acidic and sweet molasses, aromatic spices and delicious pink livers. These are all strong flavours, but pretty nice together.

CHICKEN LIVERS WITH SEVEN SPICE AND POMEGRANATE MOLASSES

SERVES 4

250g chicken livers, cleaned, any sinew removed

sea salt

olive oil

1 tsp Lebanese Seven Spice (see page 182)

knob of unsalted butter

1 tbsp pomegranate molasses

1 tbsp yogurt

1 batch of Grilled Yeasted Flatbread (see page 185)

Heat a wide pan, season the chicken livers with salt, then splash some olive oil into the pan followed by the livers. Fry without touching them for a minute until browned on one side, then turn them all over and sprinkle with the seven spice. Add the butter followed by the pomegranate molasses. Add the spoonful of yogurt, but only half stir it in before serving with the warm bread.

CLAMS COOKED IN SHERRY WITH A LITTLE PANCETTA

SERVES 4

glug of good oil

1 garlic clove, green sprout removed, finely chopped

3 thin slices pancetta, finely cut

400g carpet-shell (palourde) clams, well washed

100ml fino sherry

Heat a wide pan with a lid over a medium heat, pour in a little olive oil followed by the garlic and pancetta, then fry for a few seconds until slightly frazzled.

Add the clams followed by the fino and the lid. Cook quickly for a couple of minutes until the clams are open. Eat immediately, with bread on the table.

SMALL FISH WITH LEBANESE TARATOR

SERVES 4

1kg fresh anchovies, tiny red mullet or other small fish

600ml whole milk

1 small garlic clove, green sprout removed

sea salt

1 tbsp pine nuts

4 allspice berries

4 tbsp tahini

juice of 1 lemon

olive oil

1.5 litres sunflower oil, to deep-fry

200g semolina flour

Wash the fish. If they are fresh and small I don't usually bother to gut them (particularly anchovies), though if they are a little large you'd want to. Soak the fish in the milk.

To make the tarator, crush the garlic with a little salt, add the pine nuts and allspice and grind to a paste, followed by the tahini, then the lemon juice. It will turn very stiff, so add water until the mixture is the consistency of thick cream, then finish with a glug of olive oil.

Heat a large pan of sunflower oil to 180°C (350°F). Transfer the fish from the milk into a large bowl and cover in semolina. Deep-fry the fish in the oil in batches, until golden and crispy. Serve in piles, well salted, with the sauce alongside.

FENNEL WITH PORCINI

SERVES 4

25g dried porcini

4 fennel bulbs

50ml olive oil

4 garlic cloves, halved and green sprouts removed

sea salt

Soak the porcini in 100ml of boiling water. Cut the fennel in half, set aside the leafy tops and discard the outer layer. Choose a heavy pan that is as small as it can be without the fennel overflowing and the lid not fitting. Heat the oil and add the garlic. Fry a tiny bit, then add the fennel. Cook over a high heat for a few minutes, until some of the fennel has started to brown. Season with salt, then add the porcini and its water (be careful; sometimes grit settles at the bottom of the bowl).

Cover and cook for about 30 minutes. The fennel should be completely soft, stir it and don't worry about mushing it up, it'll still taste great. Taste to check the seasoning, add more oil if it isn't glossy and delicious and cook with the lid off for a while if it's too wet.

This ragoût is a very good one as it includes wild mushrooms and a host of other beautiful autumn vegetables.

RAGOÛT DE LÉGUMES AUTUMN

1 red onion, finely chopped

2 garlic cloves, green sprouts removed, thinly sliced

1 celery heart, finely chopped

1 bunch of Swiss chard, stalks finely chopped and leaves roughly chopped

olive oil

2 fennel bulbs

1 ripe tomato, halved

a few sprigs of thyme

knob of unsalted butter

300g wild mushrooms (porcini, chanterelle, trompettes…), cleaned

6 waxy potatoes, peeled, cut into wedges and boiled or steamed until nearly tender

In a heavy casserole pan with a lid, slowly fry the onion, garlic, celery and chard stalks until really soft and sweet in a generous amount of olive oil. Trim the fennel of its tough outer layer and cut off the base, then cut it into wedges. Add it with the tomato, thyme and butter. Cover with the lid and cook for another few minutes.

Once the fennel has started to soften, add the mushrooms, followed by the cooked potatoes. Allow to cook for a few minutes and then take a view: it should be glossy, juicy but not wet, well-seasoned yet delicate, so adjust as necessary. A few bits of toast rubbed with garlic and doused with olive oil will be welcome additions. And wine, maybe barbera, or burgundy.

This is one of my favourite dishes, though usually not with an egg. We adjust the seasonings to suit the other parts of the plate, omitting the mint if serving with salt cod, or adding coriander with lamb chops. Sometimes I completely change the spices and it tastes very north Indian instead of, as this one does, Greek.

POTATOES, OKRA AND BAKED EGGS

200g large waxy potatoes, Cyprus or Roseval are ideal

salt

2 small red onions, thinly sliced

4 garlic cloves, green sprouts removed, cut into little chips

1 heaped tsp coriander seeds, ground

2 small hot chillies, crushed

olive oil

200g okra (the small fingers are best)

3 tomatoes, torn up

a few sprigs of mint and parsley, roughly chopped

4 eggs

Peel the potatoes and cut them into wedges. Boil them in a large pan of well-salted cold water until just soft. Preheat the oven to 200°C/400°F/gas mark 6.

Meanwhile, fry the onions with the garlic, coriander and chillies in olive oil until really soft. Cut the stalks from the okra and halve each finger, add to the onion mixture and continue to fry. Add the tomatoes and, after a few minutes, when the okra is soft and the potatoes are ready (it should be around now), add them to the pan. Add more olive oil if it doesn't look glossy enough.

Transfer the okra mixture to an ovenproof frying pan or a baking tray and stir in the herbs. Break the eggs on top. Bake for a few minutes until the whites are set and the yolks still runny.

This has become a classic dish at Dock Kitchen. You can cook it on the barbecue, wrapped in foil or banana leaves.

SEA BASS BAKED IN SEASONED COCONUT WITH SQUASH

SERVES 4

1 coconut

1 fresh green chilli

1/8 small red onion

small piece of fresh root ginger

2 handfuls of fresh curry leaves, picked from stems

a few sprigs of coriander

sea salt

3 tbsp thick yogurt

1 acorn or butternut squash

3 tbsp vegetable oil

1 tsp mustard seeds

6 large mild dried chillies

1 tsp coarsely crushed coriander seeds

2 tomatoes, torn

4 x 200g pieces wild sea bass, off the bone

Preheat the oven to 200°C/400°F/gas mark 6. Break the coconut open and prise out the flesh. Peel the brown skin from the flesh with a peeler and put the flesh in a blender. Add the green chilli, onion, ginger, half the curry leaves, the coriander and salt. Blend to a fine paste, then add the yogurt. Set aside while you prepare the squash.

Peel and chop the squash into dice about the size of playing dice. Heat a wide pan over a medium-high heat, add the vegetable oil and, once hot, add the mustard seeds. When they crackle, throw in the remaining curry leaves, then the dried chillies, followed by the coriander seeds. Add the squash and tomatoes, season with salt, then cover with a lid, reduce the heat to medium and cook slowly until the squash is soft.

Smear the coconut mixture on to the fish and place the pieces into a baking tray lined with baking parchment. Bake the fish for 15 minutes, or until you can insert a long fork easily into the flesh. Serve with the squash.

Red mullet is one of my favourite fish. It has a delicate yet distinct taste that means it can be cooked in a variety of ways: as a curry, or with strong flavours such as olives and tomatoes... it always stands up well. It also couples well with the intense umami taste of clams and the strong anise flavours of the pastis in this recipe.

RED MULLET AND CLAMS WITH FENNEL, PASTIS, POTATOES AND A BIT OF TOMATO

SERVES 4

4 large waxy potatoes

2 fennel bulbs

4 garlic cloves, green sprouts removed, thinly sliced

olive oil

sea salt

freshly ground black pepper

4 x 300g red mullet

4 bay leaves

2 ripe tomatoes

150g carpet-shell (palourde) clams

100ml pastis

Preheat the oven to 200°C/400°F/gas mark 6. Peel and thinly slice the potatoes lengthways. Trim the top from the fennel, discard the tough outside layer and slice the bulbs the same thickness as the potatoes. In a large mixing bowl, drizzle the potatoes, fennel and garlic with olive oil and toss with salt and pepper, mix well to season fully and transfer to a baking tray.

Place a piece of greaseproof paper over the tray and bake until soft (about 45 minutes). Remove from the oven and lay the fish over the potatoes, tuck the bay leaves into their cavities and tear the tomatoes over everything. Season the fish a little, tip on the clams and pour over the pastis, then a little more olive oil. Return the tray to the oven for a further 15 minutes or so until the mullet are cooked and the tomatoes soft. It's nice to have a little brown on the potatoes and bits and pieces at this point, so if it's all looking a little pale, whack the grill on for a minute or so before removing from the oven.

This recipe was inspired by a Moroccan tagine, but its taste is much more domestic than that. I imagine it is a combination that must have popped up in British cooking somewhere through history, though I have seen no record of it.

SLOW-COOKED BEEF AND QUINCE

SERVES 4

2kg short ribs of beef, on the bone

1 red onion, thinly sliced

3 tomatoes

2 large quinces, peeled, cored and quartered

6 prunes

2 cinnamon sticks

1 large, mild dried chilli

1 bottle of white wine (whatever you are drinking)

sea salt

freshly ground black pepper

Preheat the oven to 160°C/325°F/gas mark 3.

Put all the ingredients into a pan with a tight-fitting lid, season well with salt and pepper and top up with water just to cover.

Put the lid on and put in the oven for six hours. Eat with a plate of Swiss chard or spinach and a dish of potatoes.

This is a brilliant Moroccan recipe that I make with all game birds; it's also perfect with partridge, mallard or pigeon.

ROAST GROUSE WITH GRAPES, HONEY AND MOROCCAN SPICES WITH COUSCOUS

1 garlic clove, green sprout removed

1 scant tsp cumin seeds

1 heaped tsp coriander seeds

1 cinnamon stick

¼ tsp turmeric

¼ tsp mild chilli powder

1 tbsp dried rose petals (if you have them)

1 tbsp honey

juice of 1 lemon

4 tbsp olive oil

4 grouse

sea salt

4 walnut-sized pieces of unsalted butter

large bunch of grapes cut into 4 small bunches (I often use muscat or fragolini, but table grapes would be fine)

350g couscous

Crush the garlic in a mortar and pestle, then add the spices, rose petals (if using), honey, lemon and half the olive oil and crush to a paste. Rub this all over the grouse, cover and marinate for a few hours in the fridge if you can; however it will still have good flavour if you don't have the time.

Preheat the oven to 220°C/425°F/gas mark 7. In a roasting tray (preferably ceramic) place all the grouse with a bit of space around each, season with salt and put a walnut of butter on each one. Roast for 10 minutes, then add the grapes and half a wine glass of water.

Roast for another six to 10 minutes, then remove from the oven and rest the birds for 10 minutes more. The birds should be pink but not bluey-red. Pull a leg away from the breast to check and just pop them back in the oven if they are underdone.

While the birds are resting, prepare the couscous by rubbing in the remaining olive oil and a good pinch of salt. Next pour over boiling water to just over 1cm above the level of the couscous. After a few minutes, when it is cool enough to touch, rub the couscous between your hands to separate the grains, making it fluffy and soft.

Put the couscous on a large serving plate and place the birds, grapes and the juices from the roasting tray on top.

We make a lot of pilaf, sometimes with artichokes, nuts, asparagus or peas. Pilaf is found throughout the Middle East. The Moghuls brought it to India where it became pilau and then biriani. There is a real art to making fluffy pilaf. You must buy good rice, soak it for a long time and wash it well. Once soaked, the rice must be treated gently; too much stirring will cause the grains to break and go stodgy, like a risotto. The aim of cooking a fluffy pilaf is almost the exact opposite of a creamy, al dente risotto.

TOMATO AND PINE NUT PILAF WITH CHICKEN LIVERS

SERVES 6

400g basmati rice

1 red onion, thinly sliced

75g unsalted butter

1 tsp allspice berries, crushed

1 cinnamon stick

3 tsp pine nuts

sea salt

freshly ground black pepper

250g canned whole plum tomatoes, washed of their juice

a few handfuls of dill, parsley and mint, leaves picked from stems

a little mild olive oil

400g chicken livers, cleaned, any sinew removed

1 tsp Lebanese Seven Spice (see page 182)

1 tbsp pomegranate molasses

250ml thick yogurt, plus more to serve

Soak the rice in warm water for two hours, then rinse well and drain.

In a heavy-based pan with a tight-fitting lid, fry the onion in the butter with the spices for 15 minutes until sweet, then add the nuts and cook for a further five minutes.

Season the base well and add the tomatoes, cook for a few minutes, then tip in the rice and mix well. Increase the heat to get the rice quite hot and add boiling water to 3cm above the level of the rice. Cook over a high heat for five minutes, a low heat for a further five, then remove from the heat and leave untouched for at least another five minutes for the grains to soften but remain separate and fluffy. Roughly chop the herbs and mix them through the pilaf.

Meanwhile, heat a frying pan over a high heat for a few minutes, add the oil and then the chicken livers. Let them brown, then turn each one over. Season with salt and sprinkle with the seven spice. When browned on both sides, add the pomegranate molasses and then a spoonful of yogurt, mix a little then remove to a serving plate. Serve the pilaf on plates and pass around the dish of livers and more yogurt if needed.

I make this often in the winter, but it is also delicious in the summer. On the odd occasion I saw Ruthie at River Café roast a chicken, she always put a splash of milk in it. I have adopted this practice; the way the milk splits and the curds brown is really special. Try to find a strong, lean, long-legged breed of chicken, not one of those flabby specimens you find in the supermarket. I like to cook a chicken off the bone, especially for this recipe, as you can get all the flavours into the flesh. It cooks faster, too.

CHICKEN ROASTED IN MILK AND SAGE

SERVES 4–6

1 large chicken, off the bone

sea salt

freshly ground black pepper

bunch of sage

olive oil

1 head of garlic

200ml whole milk

1 lemon, peeled with a vegetable peeler

2 large dried chillies

Preheat the oven to 220°C/425°F/gas mark 7. Lay the chicken out flat in a roasting tray. Season well with salt and pepper and tuck the sage leaves in and around the bird. Drizzle with olive oil, then break the head of garlic into cloves and scatter them in the tray.

Roast for 15 minutes until the skin has browned, then remove from the oven, add the milk, lemon zest and dried chillies, reduce the oven temperature to 180°C/350°F/gas mark 4 and roast for 20 minutes until cooked.

Skirt steak is an excellent, cheap cut. It must be well hung, or it will be tough. Skirt has a coarse grain and must be cooked rare; well done it is inedibly chewy. I cooked this when Jay Rayner reviewed Dock Kitchen in the early days, he said the addition of anchovy to the cauliflower cheese was the prosaic made gloriously elegiac. I was lucky to add the anchovies. Without, the excellent review may have read rather differently. This is super-simple as I just enrich crème fraîche rather than making béchamel.

GRILLED SKIRT STEAK WITH ANCHOVY CAULIFLOWER CHEESE

SERVES 4

sea salt

1 cauliflower

250ml crème fraîche

3 egg yolks

100g pecorino (or another hard tangy cheese), grated

8 salted anchovy fillets

4 skirt steaks (total weight 1kg)

freshly ground black pepper

lemon juice (optional)

extra virgin olive oil (optional)

Preheat the oven to 200°C/400°F/gas mark 6. Preheat a griddle pan, or light your barbecue.

Boil a pan of well-salted water. Break the cauliflower into florets and boil until just soft (about five minutes). Drain and put the cauliflower into a medium baking tray that can accommodate it all in one tight layer.

Mix the crème fraîche with the egg yolks and cheese and dollop this on top of the cauliflower. Lay the anchovies over the top and bake in the oven until well browned.

Season the steaks well with salt and pepper and grill on the very hot griddle pan or barbecue for a couple of minutes on each side. It should be nicely charred but still bright red within. Let them rest for a couple of minutes. I often squeeze over a lemon and pour on a little oil.

WINTER

This soup was only on the menu once at Dock Kitchen. It is aromatic and delicate. Our most regular customer, Idris, requested a reappearance of it many times, but for some reason I see it as a beautiful moment in cooking and haven't made it again for the menu. Make it if you have some fennel flowers; you can often find these growing wild, or grow some fennel herb and let it go to seed.

RED MULLET AND FENNEL SOUP

2 x 400g red mullet

1 fennel bulb, trimmed and roughly chopped

1 small red onion, roughly chopped

1 head of celery with leaves, roughly chopped

2 garlic cloves, green sprouts removed, halved

sea salt

olive oil, plus more to serve

500g whole plum tomatoes from a jar or a can, washed of their juice

2 glasses dry white wine (I use rolle)

250g small carpet-shell (palourde) clams

1 bunch fennel herb, with flowers and fresh seeds (if you can't get this, use parsley)

Fillet the mullet (or get the fishmonger to do this for you, though you'll need the bones and heads) and cut each fillet into two strips, carefully cutting down either side of the strip of tiny pin bones in the middle and removing them. Refrigerate the fillets and wash the bones well, pulling out and discarding the gills from inside the head.

In a large, heavy-based pan over a medium heat, slowly fry the fennel bulb, onion, celery and garlic, seasoned well with salt, in the olive oil for about 15 minutes, stirring occasionally, until the onion is soft and sweet. Add the mullet bones and heads and the tomatoes, fry for another few minutes then add the wine and 1 litre of water. Simmer gently for 15 minutes.

Strain through a sieve, pushing through the cooked vegetables to make a delicate, red broth. Set aside.

When you are ready to eat, heat up the broth, then add the mullet fillets and clams, cover and cook gently for a couple of minutes until the clams open. Finish with the fennel leaves, flowers and fresh seeds. Serve with toast rubbed with a cut garlic clove and olive oil.

Though I have eaten this soup countless times in Tuscany and made hundreds of pots of it at the River Café and Dock Kitchen, it is still my favourite. So it needed to be included. If you are ever in an oil-producing area between October and Christmas, look for bright green, freshly pressed olive oil. The best are pressed with high tech machinery that prevents the oil from heating or oxidising, using slightly underripe olives so the oil is grassy, spicy and green. This is delicious with a glass of chianti.

RIBOLLITA

1 red onion, finely chopped
2 carrots, finely chopped
1 head of celery, roughly chopped
sea salt
freshly ground black pepper
3 tbsp olive oil
2 large heads of cavolo nero, washed, leaves stripped from stems
3 canned whole plum tomatoes, washed of their juice
250g cooked borlotti or cannellini beans (a good can or jar is fine)
250g stale bread, crust removed, broken into chunks
lots of new season's olive oil, to pour over the soup

In a heavy-based pan, fry the onion, carrots and celery, seasoned well with salt and pepper, in the olive oil gently for a long time until totally cooked, really soft, sweet, slightly brown and full of rich flavour (this might take 45 minutes).

Add the roughly chopped cavolo nero and a glass of water and continue cooking slowly until the cavolo is completely soft. If you need to, add more water to stop it from frying. Add the tomatoes, torn a little with your hands and the beans (rinsed well if using canned).

Add a little more water, cook together for about five minutes and adjust the seasoning. Place the bread on top of the thick soup mixture and push the chunks down with a wooden spoon; when the bread has softened into the soup, stir to break it up. Loosen with a little water to make a thick, rich soup. Let it sit for a little while before you eat and don't eat it too hot. Generously pour olive oil on the top as you serve it.

Often on Chinese restaurant menus this is translated as gruel, which obviously puts most people off. It is a delicious and comforting dish often eaten for breakfast, though we usually serve it for lunch.

DUCK AND MUSHROOM CONGEE

150g jasmine rice

2 duck legs, each cut into 2 (thighs and drumsticks)

4 dried Chinese mushrooms

2cm fresh root ginger, grated

2 star anise

1 cinnamon stick

1 large dried chilli

a few coriander leaves, to serve

handful of beansprouts, to serve (optional)

Put all the ingredients except the coriander leaves and beansprouts into a heavy-based pan with a tight-fitting lid and pour in 1.5 litres of water. Set the pan over a medium heat. When it comes to a boil, reduce the heat to its lowest setting and cook for about 1½ hours.

When the duck is soft, pull the flesh from the bone, discard the skin and bones and return it to the pan.

Serve the congee with a little coriander and a handful of beansprouts, if you have them.

This is suited to summer or winter, though it was on the winter menu at Dock Kitchen for a while. Sometimes I make this plate a bit bigger, adding a little pile of clams and some tiny roast fish so it becomes a beautiful starter to share. This makes more than the other toasts recipes in this book, but that's because there's little point in cooking a half or a quarter of a frozen octopus...

THREE LITTLE TOASTS FOR WINTER: OCTOPUS, CRAB AND COOKED ROCKET

SERVES 10

For the toasts

good olive oil

10 large slices of coarse sourdough bread

1 garlic clove

For the octopus

1 octopus (I usually buy a frozen Spanish one)

1 head of garlic

glass of white wine

400g can of whole plum tomatoes, washed of their juice

1 tbsp fennel seeds

For the crab

sea salt

freshly ground black pepper

500g crab meat, white and brown

1 small hot chilli, crushed

1 tsp fennel seeds, roughly ground

¼ garlic clove, crushed with salt in a mortar and pestle

1 lemon

For the rocket

2 garlic cloves, green sprouts removed, very thinly sliced

500g rocket, roughly chopped

Preheat the oven to 180°C/350°F/gas mark 4. Bake the octopus with the garlic, wine, tomatoes and fennel seeds for about 1 hour until soft, but still a little bit chewy; you'll have to cut a bit off to see. Octopus can take hours to cook or just 45 minutes, so make sure you leave a good bit of time.

When it's ready, cut the legs into 1cm slices and the head into little rings. Discard the hard bit at the top of the legs (the beak) and the mush inside the head. Mix the octopus with a little bit of the cooked garlic and tomato, mushed up a bit, then pour over a little olive oil to make a rich delicious mixture. If there is a lot of liquid still in the tray, freeze it or keep it in the fridge, as it will make the most amazing addition to a fish stew or risotto.

Season the crab, mix the brown and white meat together, add the chilli, fennel seeds and garlic, generously dress with olive oil and lemon juice and taste to check lemon and salt.

Next prepare the rocket. Fry the garlic in a large pan in a generous amount of olive oil until it just starts to brown and slightly stick together. Add the rocket and a splash of water if it is not wet, cook for a few minutes until the leaves are soft, season and set aside.

When you are ready to eat, grill the bread on a heavy cast-iron griddle pan until quite dark and crunchy, then rub each one gently with the cut garlic clove. You'll have to move pretty fast so everyone doesn't get cold toast. Cut the pieces into three and top 10 of each with a different topping.

A thoran is one of the most delicious and imaginative ways to eat the best vegetables of the season, and so very good.

THORAN OF WHITE CABBAGE AND CARROTS

SERVES 4

2 tbsp flavourless oil (I use a neutral olive oil)

1 tsp mustard seeds

3 large mild dried chillies, chopped

handful of fresh curry leaves, picked from stems

½ tsp finely ground black pepper

3 carrots, diced

¼ white cabbage, diced

½ small sweet red onion, diced

salt

100g fresh coconut, finely grated

Heat a large frying pan with the oil and tip in the mustard seeds until they crackle. Then add the chillies and curry leaves for a few seconds, then the black pepper.

When everything is popping, add the carrots, cabbage and onion, season with salt and cook together for a few more minutes.

Mix in the grated coconut, then taste and check the seasoning. Eat hot with White or Brown Chapati (see page 183).

MOROCCAN SALADS

Posh meals in Morocco always start with salads; they can be incredibly varied and are always very exotic. Often quite sweet, sometimes also sour, usually with flower water, they feel cleansing and fresh, setting you up for the richer, slow-cooked meats to follow. I make a few as a starter on the lunch menu at Dock Kitchen.

CARROT AND ORANGE SALAD

2 oranges (I use blood oranges when in season)
4 carrots, coarsely grated
large pinch of toasted ground cumin
½ lemon
orange flower water
caster sugar (optional)

Peel the oranges with a knife, removing both skin and pith. Cut them in half, then slice into thin half moons.

Mix the carrots with the oranges and cumin. Squeeze over the lemon and sprinkle with a few drops of orange flower water. Taste, add a little sugar if needed, depending on the sweetness of the oranges.

CUCUMBER SALAD

2 small cucumbers
sea salt
leaves from a few sprigs of mint
1 tsp caster sugar
squeeze of lemon
a few drops of rose water

Coarsely grate the cucumbers, season with salt, toss and let sit in a sieve to remove some of their liquid for about 20 minutes.

Move into a bowl and add the mint leaves, season with sugar, lemon and rose water, taste as you do it and build up the flavours, it should be refreshing, yet the delicate aroma of the cucumber should still be present.

CHICKEN LIVER SALAD

2 tbsp olive oil
150g chicken livers, cleaned, any sinew removed
sea salt
1 tsp ground toasted cumin
a few tomatoes from a can or jar, washed of their juice
leaves from small bunch of coriander, roughly chopped
½ tsp ground cinnamon

Heat a small frying pan, add the olive oil and then the chicken livers, season with salt then sprinkle with the cumin. When lightly brown on one side, turn over and tear the tomatoes into the pan, cook for another couple of minutes, then stir in the coriander and cinnamon.

Eat warm or room temperature; the livers should be slightly pink inside.

BEETROOT SALAD

4 golf ball-sized beetroots

sea salt

1 tbsp blanched almonds, toasted

1 small garlic clove, green sprout removed

splash of cider vinegar or good red wine vinegar

a few drops of rose water

olive oil

½ tsp caraway seeds

Boil the beetroots in well-salted water until soft, but not as soft as a cooked potato. Drain and set aside to cool. Remove the skin with your hands and cut the beetroots into little wedges.

Crush the nuts roughly in a mortar and pestle, then add the garlic with a little salt and crush to a fine white paste. Mix the beetroots, nut mixture, vinegar, rose water and olive oil together with the caraway. Taste and adjust the balance, it should be well rounded.

MARINATED OLIVES

2 garlic cloves, green sprouts removed

250g large, firm, green olives

½ a preserved lemon, finely chopped

handful of celery leaves (the yellow ones from the centre of the heart), roughly chopped

2 large chillies, roughly chopped

pinch of toasted ground cumin

¼ tsp paprika

a few sprigs of coriander, leaves picked from stems and roughly chopped

100ml good olive oil

Squash the garlic cloves a bit and put them in a bowl with the olives. Add the preserved lemon, celery leaves, chillies, cumin, paprika and coriander. Mix all together and add the olive oil.

Let the olives sit for as long as you can, but they are also pretty good eaten immediately.

This is a classic Moroccan dish. The warka pastry is a bit tricky to make, but if you fancy doing it there's a great description of how to go about it in *Moro, the Cookbook*. Squab pigeons are delicately flavoured but more expensive; wood pigeons are drier and gamier in taste. You could also make this with chicken legs or rabbit. It's quite a big job, but worth it.

PIGEON PASTILLA

150g unsalted butter

3 pigeons

3 red onions, thinly sliced

½ bunch of coriander

½ bunch of parsley

pinch of saffron threads

1 tbsp honey, plus more if needed

1 cinnamon stick

sea salt

150g blanched almonds, toasted and roughly chopped

6 eggs

splash of orange flower water

1kg large filo sheets, or warka pastry

2 tbsp icing sugar

1 tbsp ground cinnamon

In a wide pan, melt 100g of the butter, then add the pigeons, onions, the herbs tied into a bunch, the saffron, honey and cinnamon stick. Cover with water, season well with salt and cook over a low heat for an hour.

Remove the pigeons and increase the heat to reduce the mixture while you remove all the meat from the bones of the birds. Shred the meat a little and return to the pan. Discard the herb bunch and cook until the liquid is just below the level of everything else.

Add the almonds. Break the eggs into a bowl and gently whisk, pour two-thirds into the pigeon mixture and stir, cooking over a medium heat for a few minutes until you have little bits of cooked egg through the mixture. Taste, add a little more salt or honey to get it tasting full, sweet, savoury and exotic. Add a splash of orange flower water. Set aside to cool. Fish out the cinnamon stick.

Preheat the oven to 150°C/300°F/gas mark 2.

Melt the remaining butter. Lay three pastry sheets out on wide soup bowls and butter lightly with a pastry brush. Repeat twice to make three layers, buttering as you go.

Using a slotted spoon, put one-third of the pigeon mixture on to each of the filo piles – leaving the excess liquid behind – and wrap them up into round parcels, tucking the edges back over the bottom of the pie. Paint with any remaining butter and the last of the egg to seal.

Transfer to a baking tray and bake for 45 minutes until crisp and brown. Dust with icing sugar and cinnamon (usually in a lattice pattern) and eat hot.

This is an ubiquitous Lebanese small plate, served all over the country with different toppings, from minced lamb and onions to dried yogurt or a delicious mixture of nuts, garlic and chillies. I love za'atar, it's a mixture of loads of wild herbs, dried and chopped up together. Mankoush is sometimes cooked in a wood-fired oven, or in a big inverted cast-iron wok-like thing on top of an open fire.

MANKOUSH

1 batch Yeasted Flatbread dough (see page 185), split into 6 balls, plus more strong white flour to dust

100g za'atar

40ml olive oil, plus more to serve

coarse sea salt

handful of semolina, or more strong white flour

250g labne (see page 19)

pickled chillies, cucumbers or salted olives

sprigs of mint, parsley, dill and tarragon

Preheat the oven to its highest setting. Roll each dough ball out on a lightly floured surface into round discs about 3mm thick. Make holes in the bread with a fork. Set aside while you prepare the za'atar mixture.

In a small bowl, mix the za'atar with the olive oil and some coarse salt into a thick paste. Spread the mixture thickly on the dough. Dust a heavy metal tray with the semolina or flour and place on the mankoush. Bake for about five minutes, or until light brown and starting to go crunchy.

Serve with a bowl of labne with olive oil poured over it, a few pickles and a pile of fresh, sweet herbs.

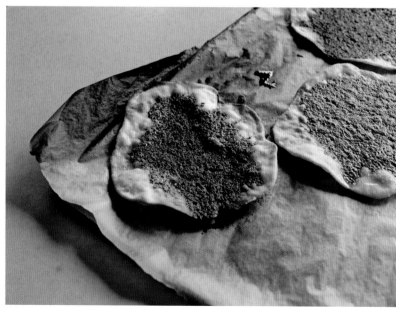

As with ribollita, this dish is all about the amazing combination of fresh oil and cavolo nero. Rose at the River Café taught me to wait until the cavolo has had a hard frost before cutting it, as the starches change and become sweeter. Choose large, robust bunches. Try to find fresh ricotta rather than the long-life sort they sell in the supermarket. If the long-life type is all you can find, season it well with salt, pepper and Parmesan and mix with olive oil. This dish is very simple and very delicious.

CAVOLO NERO, NEW OIL, BRUSCHETTA

SERVES 4

2 large bunches of cavolo nero

4 garlic cloves

sea salt

4 thick slices of good, open-textured sourdough or semolina bread

200g fresh buffalo's or sheep's ricotta

new season's olive oil

Strip the leaves from the stalks of the cavolo nero. Put a large pan of water over a high heat with three of the garlic cloves and lots of salt. Boil the water until the garlic is completely soft, then add the cavolo. Continue to boil until the cabbage is completely soft, it will take about 10 minutes. Drain the cabbage and check the seasoning.

Toast the bread, preferably on a chargrill, until hard and dark. Rub confidently three times with the remaining, halved garlic clove, then top with cavolo and a big blob of ricotta. Eat immediately, with loads of green oil poured over the top.

My grandfather used to make devils on horseback, I love the salty bacon with the sweet prunes. My friend April at the Spotted Pig in New York puts a piece of pickled pear inside. New Yorkers are crazy for Devils these days and you see them in bars all over the place. I use pancetta as it usually slices thinner and crisps better than thicker cut English streaky.

DEVILS ON HORSEBACK

50ml red wine vinegar

2 bay leaves

6 juniper seeds

1 dried chilli

1 Earl Grey tea bag

20 prunes d'Agen

20 blanched almonds, slightly toasted

20 thin slices of pancetta

Heat a pan of water large enough to submerge your prunes in. Add the vinegar, bay, juniper and dried chilli and simmer for five minutes. Remove from the heat, add the tea bag and prunes and leave for a few hours, or even overnight.

Drain the prunes, but keep a bit of the liquid. Remove the stones from the prunes and push in an almond, then roll the little parcel up tightly with a piece of pancetta.

When you are ready to cook them, preheat a grill to its highest setting. Lay the devils out in a tray where they fit tightly and pour on a little of the soaking liquid. Roast under a low grill, turning occasionally, until hot, crispy, sticky and delicious.

Eat with warm, yeasty ale.

This is my version of a salad traditionally eaten on Christmas Eve in Mexico. The country is full of delicious varieties of chilli, often sun-dried, smoked or pickled, the parade is seemingly endless. Thankfully, due in no small part to my friend Tommi Miers' hard work at her restaurant chain Wahaca, these chillies are becoming more and more easily available outside Mexico. This salad requires a lot of chopping; you could employ the aid of a mezzaluna but never a Magimix.

ENSALADA DE LA NOCHE BUENA

SERVES 4

2 tbsp olive oil

1 tsp chipotle flakes

2 fennel bulbs, trimmed and finely diced

seeds from 1 pomegranate

1 green chilli, finely chopped

1/8 small red onion, finely diced

small bunch of coriander, roughly chopped

small bunch of radishes, roughly chopped

1 blood orange (or good-flavoured regular orange), sections roughly chopped

juice of 2–4 limes, depending how juicy they are

sea salt

Heat the olive oil in a saucepan and add the chipotle flakes. Cook over a medium heat for a couple of minutes until the aroma from the chillies is strong but they haven't yet become dark and bitter. If you burn them start again, chillies burn suddenly as they contain quite a lot of sugar.

Mix the fennel, pomegranate, green chilli, onion, coriander, radishes and orange together in a bowl. Take a view. You need to think about balance, sometimes the fennel bulbs are small or you lost a lot of orange when you peeled it, add whatever you think you need to achieve a crunchy, zingy, sweet and sour salad.

Dress with the chipotle and its oil, the lime and salt, then taste again and adjust the acidity and seasoning. Eat soon, though this salad will hold for about 30 minutes, which is longer than its softer comrades.

I love fattoush, the ubiquitous Lebanese salad of tomatoes, cucumbers, purslane and crispbread, but because I cook with the seasons I used not to make it in winter. Then I was cooking a Lebanese meal and decided it needed something to fill the fattoush gap. This evolved, using pomegranate molasses to add depth to the usual lemon/sumac combo and celery, fennel and herbs instead of tomatoes and cucumbers. It should be fresh tasting and acidic, dressed with less oil than you would a normal mixed salad.

A KIND OF WINTER FATTOUSH

SERVES 4

100ml olive oil

1 pitta bread

2 fennel bulbs, thinly sliced

1 celery heart, thinly sliced

seeds from 1 pomegranate

leaves from a few sprigs of parsley

handful of small sweet spinach leaves

leaves from a few sprigs of mint

¼ good, unwaxed lemon, plus more if needed

1 tsp pomegranate molasses

½ tsp sumac

3 tbsp good olive oil

sea salt

Heat the olive oil in a small pan, cut the pitta into long strips, then fry it until crispy. Remove from the pan and place on kitchen paper.

Mix the fennel, celery and pomegranate seeds together. Roughly chop the parsley and spinach and add them too, then tear the mint into the bowl. Thinly slice the lemon into thin triangular slices and put these into the bowl. Add the pomegranate molasses, fried pitta bread, sumac and the good olive oil.

Season well with salt and taste for seasoning and acidity, adding a squeeze of lemon if you think it needs it.

We cook clams at Dock Kitchen all the time, this is one of the best ones. The riesling really stands up well to the clams, cinnamon and chilli. Choose a dry one that you would like to drink, there are some great bottles coming from the New World as well as the more traditional Alsace region. There's quite a lot of butter here (which is unusual for me) but the sauce is lovely and rich and glossy, use less if you're worried about your heart.

CLAMS COOKED IN BUTTER, RIESLING AND CINNAMON   SERVES 4–6

100g unsalted butter

2 garlic cloves, green sprouts removed, cut into little chips

1 large mild dried chilli (such as Kashmiri)

10cm cinnamon stick, broken up a bit

500g carpet-shell (palourde) clams

large glass of the riesling you are drinking

Heat a large heavy-based pan (not too hot that it will burn the butter), add half the butter, the garlic, then the chilli and cinnamon. When it begins to soften and the aroma fills the air, add the clams and riesling, increase the heat and put on the lid.

Cook fast for a few minutes until the clams start to open. Remove the lid, add the remaining butter and cook for another few minutes to allow the juices to reduce and mix with the butter to form a rich, glossy sauce. Some good bread and the rest of the bottle of wine will set you up well.

This is a Spanish Catalan dish. I love the strong flavours of slowly browned garlic, smoked paprika and sherry vinegar.

SARDINES IN ESCABECHE

12 sardines, butterflied
50ml olive oil
12 garlic cloves
1 tsp hot smoked paprika
6 bay leaves
200ml sherry vinegar

In a large frying pan, briefly fry the sardines skin side down in a little bit of the olive oil; just frazzle the skin, don't cook them all the way through. Lay them out on a plate and set aside.

Add the rest of the olive oil to the pan and reduce the heat. Add the whole garlic cloves and fry very gently until completely soft, then increase the heat and cook them until starting to go crisp and golden brown.

Once the garlic has browned, add the paprika, bay leaves and quickly, before the paprika burns, with the pan off the heat, add the vinegar. Return to the heat and cook for another few minutes. Pour this lovely mixture over the sardines and let them sit for an hour or so or until you are ready to eat. You'll want a little salad (perhaps raw fennel) and some pieces of toast with them.

THOUGHTS ON FISH

I am very careful about buying my fish, either for home or my restaurant, as I worry a lot about quality and also sustainability.

Luckily, quality in fish is actually quite easy to assess. Fish need to look as though they are healthy and almost still alive. Bright sparkling eyes, red gills and firm, toned flesh (as in the photo above) are the signs of a delicious fresh fish.

It is still rare to find a truly beautiful farmed fish. They tend to be flabby specimens – having had no chance to swim for dear life in a rough icy sea in search of food – their fins often tattered, having been eaten by the other fish trapped in the farms with them. Hook-nosed and deformed, farmed fish have a hard life, covered in lice and worms and sprayed for treatment. Salmon seems to be the worst of all the farmed fish. Fed on really destructively caught fish meal, it tastes horrible too and is incredibly fatty when you cook it.

There seem to be a few farms who are producing healthy fish, using sustainable fish food. This really seems to be something we should be supporting; fish stocks are low and sustainable solutions to plundering the sea need to be found.

As a general rule, if your fish is caught in a low-impact way – line-caught not dredged – it is sustainable. However, in reality it is rather more complex than that. Varieties of fish from some waters have become endangered while in other fisheries they can be quite common.

At some times of year it is best to avoid certain fish in roe. I find it safest to consult the Marine Stewardship Council website (msc.org) if I am unsure, as they have the most up-to-date information on where your fish should be coming from and the methods by which it should be caught, as well as advising which species we should be avoiding completely.

We make our own coconut milk for all coconut-based curries. It is delicate, tasty and elegant. If you want to use canned, water it down a bit as it is far too thick and rich. Fresh curry leaves are delicious. Find a shop that stocks them (or convince one to); they can seriously improve your quality of life. Buy a few packets when you see them and put them in the freezer

BRILL AND COCONUT MOILEE

SERVES 4

1 small butternut or onion squash, peeled and cut into 2.5cm wedges

sea salt

2 tbsp mild olive or vegetable oil

small bunch of fresh curry leaves, picked from stems

1 tsp black mustard seeds

2 tsp ground coriander

½ tsp ground fenugreek seeds

1 tsp finely ground black pepper

½ tsp turmeric

½ tsp ground fennel seeds

1 tsp whole cardamom pods

1 small cinnamon stick

2 small, sweet red onions, thinly sliced

2 garlic cloves, green sprouts removed, cut into little chips

1 large red chilli, finely sliced

2.5cm fresh root ginger, finely chopped

2 coconuts, flesh removed from shell and peeled

6 large pieces of brill, cut on the bone

200g canned whole plum tomatoes, washed of their juice

Put the pieces of squash in a saucepan of well-salted water, bring to a boil, reduce the heat and simmer until almost soft. Drain and set aside.

In a wide shallow pan over a high heat, heat the oil and add the curry leaves. When they crackle, add the spices and then straightaway the onions, garlic, chilli and ginger. Reduce the heat right down to fry gently, making a tasty, sweet, spiced base for the curry.

Meanwhile, make the coconut milk. Finely grate the coconut flesh, add 1 litre of boiling water and let sit for 10 minutes, then pour through a sieve and squeeze the coconut to release the thicker coconut milk.

Add the fish and squash to the cooking spices, tear in the tomatoes, then pour over the coconut milk, season and gently cook for 10 minutes, or until the fish pulls easily from the bone.

Serve with a bowl of warm rice or a few White or Brown Chapati (see page 183).

I like to put a big fish roast over potatoes on the menu to share for Sunday lunch. John Dory is my favourite for this. I distinctly remember eating this on a family holiday on the Tuscan coast as a child.

WHOLE JOHN DORY ROAST OVER POTATOES

SERVES 6

500g large waxy potatoes

4 large fennel bulbs

4 garlic cloves, green sprouts removed, thinly sliced

olive oil

sea salt

freshly ground black pepper

2 glasses of vermentino, or another dry white with good acidity

2kg whole John Dory

a few large sprigs of rosemary

Preheat the oven to 200°C/400°F/gas mark 6. Peel and slice the potatoes about 1cm thick. Remove the outer layer of the fennel and then slice it the same thickness as the potato. In a large bowl, mix the potatoes, fennel and garlic together, generously pour over olive oil and season well with salt and pepper.

Put this mixture into a tray. Pour over one glass of wine and seal with foil.

Bake for 30–40 minutes until the potatoes and fennel are both soft. Remove from the oven and lay the fish on top. Turn the oven temperature up to as hot as it will go. Season the fish outside and in the cavity, tuck in the branches of rosemary and pour over another glass of wine. Roast for about 20 minutes, or until the fish pulls easily from the bone.

This ragoût calls for beautiful vegetables: proper carrots, fresh artichokes, fennel... vary the vegetables with availability. Some of my favourite vegetables come into season in the winter; there's a surprising variety even when the garden is seemingly bare.

RAGOÛT DE LÉGUMES WINTER

SERVES 6

3 large or 6 small artichokes
1 lemon, halved
1 large red onion
50g unsalted butter
a few sprigs of thyme
3 garlic cloves, green sprouts removed, sliced
3 fennel bulbs, trimmed and cut into wedges
3 muddy carrots, cut into wedges
1 celery heart, cut into 10cm pieces
about 100ml white wine

Peel off the artichoke leaves from the base until the leaves are paler green and tender about halfway up their length. Cut the tips of the leaves off at the point where the leaf becomes tough. Peel the dark green part from the stalks and heart to reveal the soft, pale green heart. Cut the artichokes in half and scoop out the furry choke, then rub them with lemon to prevent discolouration and set aside. Boil a small pan of water and boil the artichoke pieces for five minutes to soften.

Slice the onion and fry in the butter with the thyme and garlic in a heavy-based pan with a tight-fitting lid that will accommodate all the vegetables.

Add the fennel, carrots and celery and cover, reduce the heat and allow to steam. Once they start to soften, add the artichokes and a splash of white wine. Continue to cook, covered, until all the vegetables are soft and tasty.

We make pilaf often at Dock Kitchen. This is one of the best winter ones. Try to find a good, aged Himalayan basmati. Tilda is a good basic brand.

CAULIFLOWER PILAF

300g good-quality white basmati rice

2 red onions, sliced

150g unsalted butter

sea salt

1 heaped tsp allspice, freshly ground (or some allspice and Baghdad Bharat, see page 182)

2.5cm cinnamon stick

1 tsp black cumin seeds (if you don't have any omit it, don't use brown cumin as it's very different)

1 tsp coriander seeds, ground

1 large handsome fresh cauliflower with a few leaves attached

3 garlic cloves, green sprouts removed

handful of cashew nuts

small tub of good yogurt

large handful of chopped sweet herbs (dill, parsley, mint, tarragon and marjoram all qualify; use at least half parsley though), chopped

Soak the rice in warm water for two hours.

In a heavy-based saucepan with a tight-fitting lid, fry the onions in the butter very slowly. Add enough salt to season the whole dish, then add all the spices.

Break the cauliflower into florets, keeping the tender leaves attached and boil in salted water until it begins to soften. Drain and set aside.

When the onions are just starting to be soft and sweet, add two of the garlic cloves, finely chopped, and the cashew nuts. Fry gently until the onions have completely broken down.

Rinse the basmati until the water runs clear, then drain well. Increase the heat under the onions and add the cauliflower. When it is nicely coated in the spices, add the drained rice and fry until it is all hot and sizzling. Cover with boiling water or stock if you have some; make sure the liquid covers the rice by a little more than 1cm. Cover with a piece of greaseproof paper and the lid, then cook over a high heat for about five minutes. Reduce the heat to low for another five minutes. Remove from the heat but leave undisturbed for at least five minutes more.

Meanwhile, crush the remaining garlic clove and mix it into the yogurt. When the pilaf has rested, remove the lid and fluff it with a fork, add the soft herbs and eat with the seasoned yogurt.

This recipe, which is really called pigeon fesenjan, is a real celebratory Persian dish. When the brilliant Australian chef Greg Malouf came to cook at Dock Kitchen, he made a version of this with duck. We often make it with chicken, but for a special occasion it's great to use delicious (if expensive) farmed pigeons from the south of France. It's also fabulous with grouse.

PIGEON WITH POMEGRANATES AND WALNUTS

SERVES 4

250g shelled walnuts, slightly toasted and peeled

3 tbsp olive oil

1 red onion, finely diced

2 cinnamon sticks

½ tsp turmeric

½ tsp freshly ground black pepper

1 tbsp cardamom pods, crushed

125g canned whole plum tomatoes, washed of their juice, roughly chopped

2 tbsp pomegranate molasses, or to taste

250ml pomegranate juice

1 tbsp caster sugar

2 bay leaves

sea salt

freshly ground black pepper

4 Anjou pigeons

a few knobs of unsalted butter

a few sprigs of dill, tarragon, coriander mint, parsley or rocket

Grind the walnuts (be sure that they are still reasonably coarse, or the texture will be ruined). Preheat the oven to 200°C/400°F/gas mark 6.

Heat the olive oil in a large, heavy-based saucepan. Add the onion and fry gently until soft and translucent (about 10 minutes). Stir in the spices and tomatoes and fry for another 10 minutes or so, breaking up the tomatoes with the back of your spoon. Add the walnuts, pomegranate molasses and juice, sugar, bay leaves and 500ml water, season well and simmer for about 10 minutes. Taste and adjust the acidity with pomegranate molasses.

Heat a wide ovenproof pan, season the pigeons and then brown them in the butter over a medium heat. Add the pomegranate-walnut fesenjan sauce, then put the pan into the oven and roast, uncovered, for about 20 minutes. The pigeons should still be pink; just pull the leg from the breast and have a look to check.

Rest for about five minutes, then serve with the sprigs of herbs, undressed but very fresh, and the lovely Chelow Rice (see right).

There is something really special about this classic Iranian rice with its crispy base. Fun to make and lovely to eat. To cook this rice, use a good heavy-based pan with a tight lid, or the heat will not distribute evenly on the base and the steam will escape. It is delicious with slow-cooked Middle Eastern stews, or eat the crispy base with yogurt as part of a mezze.

CHELOW RICE

SERVES 4

250g basmati rice

large pinch of saffron threads

sea salt

2 tbsp olive oil

75g unsalted butter, melted

Wash the basmati rice well, then soak for at least one hour. Place the saffron in a small bowl and cover with 75ml boiling water.

After both rice and saffron have soaked, bring a large pan of well-salted water to a boil. When it is boiling, add the rice, boil fast for eight minutes, then drain into a colander. Rinse with lukewarm water and stir the rice with your hands to separate the grains.

Put a medium, heavy-based pan with a tight-fitting lid over a medium-high heat. After a few minutes, when the pan is properly hot, add the olive oil. Add the rice to the oil and, with a spoon, shape the rice into a cone with its highest point in the middle of the pan. Pour over the melted butter, cook for about five minutes until the rice is really hissing, then add the saffron water and cover with the lid. If you do not have a really tight-fitting lid, wrap the lid with a thin tea towel and weigh down with something heavy like a mortar and pestle. Reduce the heat to medium-low and cook for a further 30 minutes.

When you are ready to serve, dip the base of the hot pan into cold water. This will help to remove the crispy rice that may have stuck to the bottom. Invert the pan on to a plate and cross your fingers for good luck. When you remove the pan you should have a beautiful mound of steaming, fragrant saffron rice with a beautiful brown, crispy crust. If the shape has not quite held, cover with a clean tea towel and shape into a mound.

WELL-HUNG BEEF

There is good beef and there is bad beef.

People are always talking about hanging meat, particularly beef. Lots of people know that hanging beef is a good thing and, through various well-marketed products and boastfully worded menus, we know that hanging for 28 days is pretty good. However, not many of us know what happens to meat as it ages. Firstly, there are two types of ageing: wet and dry. As far as I understand, quality butchers only dry-age meat. Wet-ageing is just vacuum packing the meat until rigor mortis has departed (this takes about 48 hours). But only quality beef can be dry-aged. Old varieties such as Hereford, Longhorn and Angus are suitable because they grow slowly and develop a solid covering of fat. Meat from modern commercial breeds doesn't have time to develop the fat and, even if it did, significant amounts of these animals' fat have usually been bred out to suit today's tastes.

Dry-ageing beef improves flavour in three ways. Firstly it dries it out; meat can lose up to 30 per cent of its weight while ageing through water evaporation, which obviously concentrates the meat and intensifies the flavour. It also makes it more expensive; because much of the weight has evaporated, the butcher must charge more per kilo. The second boon of dry-ageing is that, as the meat hangs, enzymes naturally occurring in the beef start to break down the connective tissue, making the beef more tender, which also makes it more delicious. Finally, the process of dry-ageing allows some fungus to grow on the outside of the meat. Fungus such as thamnidia add really good flavour to meat and also break it down, helping to tenderise it. That slightly gamey taste of properly dry-aged beef is thanks to these little germs growing on the outside of the carcass.

Of course beef can be hung for too long; these days it is quite trendy. Some butchers hang meat for well over four weeks and sometimes you get meat that tastes almost cured, with far too much of the 'high' taste from the thamnidia and nothing of the taste from the beast itself.

About butchers

If you find a good butcher you should support him. Generally you can spot pretty quickly when a butcher has his priorities right. He'll be talking about the farms where his meat comes from, the breeds and the influence of the time of year or the age of the beast. His meat will look dry and beautiful. The chickens will be long-legged, small-breasted creatures with thick rough skin, while the pork will be properly covered in a beautiful, thick, clean layer of delicious white fat.

His prices will probably be quite high. Good meat is expensive. Sometimes very expensive. There are lots of reasons why, mostly because it is not intensively reared. By its nature, good meat is quite artisanal: the animals need a lot of space, good food, care and attention. The abattoirs used need to be small and local, or even on site. The increasing and ever-changing Health and Safety requirements are difficult for small producers to comply to.

I try to buy expensive meat, but eat it less often, as well as buying cheaper cuts from an expensive butcher. Well-hung beef makes the traditionally tougher cuts more tender: topside, rump and silverside from a fabulous bit of beef make for great steaks. You don't have to go for fillet and sirloin the whole time.

The butchers' shops themselves are also difficult businesses to make work. Dealing with small producers is difficult. Good butchers cope with infrequent deliveries, make a commitment to buy in advance and take delivery of whole beasts. It can be challenging.

Ease is one of the reasons that most (but not all) of the meat in my restaurant comes from butchers, not farmers. Generally I avoid the meat in farmers' markets as it tends to be vacuum-packed; farmers rarely have the ability to dry-age meat properly. Farmers are not butchers.

Good butchery is almost as important as well-reared beasts, and the skills of the butcher should not be underestimated.

At Dock Kitchen we often have a variation of this recipe on the menu. It's great to be able to put it in the oven the night before and have one of the dishes done already. It also cooks beautifully slowly overnight.

SPICED BEEF SHIN IN RED WINE

1 large beef shin (4kg)

2 bottles of red wine (I use chianti)

2 cinnamon sticks

1 tbsp fennel seeds

3 star anise

1 tbsp coarsely ground black pepper

2 dried red chillies

1 tbsp allspice

1 head of garlic, whole and unpeeled

6 bay leaves

sea salt

Preheat the oven to 130°C/266°F/gas mark ½. Put the beef in a large pan that can go both on the hob and in the oven; it needs to fit snugly or you will have to use too much liquid to submerge it.

Add the rest of the ingredients and a good handful of salt (remember that you have to season all of the meat and the liquid). Add water to cover the beef completely. Put on the lid and bake in the oven for eight hours.

I sometimes cook this dish on the hob or on top of my wood stove if the oven is busy, just make sure it doesn't bubble too fast. By the end of cooking, the meat should be completely soft and any sinew or fatty bits deliciously gloopy. Eat it with small, waxy baked potatoes. I like to scrape the bone marrow out of the bone and put it on baked potatoes or on toast.

This tastes better with lamb cooked on the bone but, if you can only find it off the bone, just use that. Stone-in prunes hold together better.

LAMB AND PRUNE TAGINE

2 large white onions, finely chopped

2 tbsp olive oil

sea salt

1.5kg lamb shoulder, shank or neck, cut into large chunks on the bone by your butcher

1 cinnamon stick

½ tsp turmeric

1 tsp finely ground black pepper

½ tsp sweet paprika (preferably unsmoked)

30 prunes, with the stones left in

Heat a large deep casserole (big enough to hold the meat in one layer) or tagine over a low heat and add the onions and olive oil. Season well with salt (add enough at this point to season the whole dish) and cook slowly until soft (about 10 minutes). Add the lamb and increase the heat a little. Continue to fry, stirring often while you add the spices. If the onions start to catch, reduce the heat.

After five more minutes all the flavours should be filling the room. Add the prunes and 400ml water. Cover with the lid and reduce the heat.

Cook gently for two hours, checking occasionally to make sure it isn't going too fast (it should be just bubbling gently). It's ready when the meat is soft, just falling off the bone. Eat with couscous.

This is a beautiful dish. The vivid colour of beetroot is always a pleasure and the earthy taste goes beautifully with the exotic spicing. A play on the classic feast dish of whole lamb stuffed with nut or artichoke pilaf that you get across much of the Middle East, this is a simpler, prettier version.

LAMB SHOULDER STUFFED WITH BEETROOT PILAF

SERVES 6

For the lamb

1 x 2.5kg boneless lamb shoulder

2 tsp ground allspice

1 tbsp pomegranate molasses

sea salt

1 head of garlic

For the pilaf

300g white basmati rice

2 red onions, sliced

150g unsalted butter

1 tsp ground allspice

1 tsp black cumin seeds

1 cinnamon stick

5 small beetroots, scrubbed and coarsely grated

small bunch of dill, chopped

few sprigs of mint

First make the pilaf. Wash the rice well, then soak it in warm water for two hours. Rinse again, until the water runs clear. Choose a medium, heavy-based pan with a lid. Fry the sliced onions in the butter and add the spices. Cook over a medium heat for about 15 minutes until completely soft. Add the beetroot and cook for a few more minutes. Add the rice, then cover with boiling water to 2cm above the level of the rice. Cook over a high heat with the lid on for three minutes, then reduce the heat to low for five minutes more. Rest the rice for another five minutes while you prepare the lamb.

Preheat the oven to 140°C/275°F/gas mark 1. Lay the lamb out on a baking tray, rub with the ground allspice, pomegranate molasses and salt, smash up the garlic a bit and rub that in too. Put half the pilaf inside the shoulder where the bone would have been, tuck the flesh around the rice and place in an oven tray. Add 2.5cm water, seal with foil and bake for three hours.

Remove the lamb from the oven and add the rest of the rice to the tray. Increase the oven temperature to 200°C/400°F/gas mark 6. Return the lamb and rice to the oven and roast for 15 minutes until the lamb is nicely brown. Serve sprinkled with the herbs, with yogurt and a plate of greens.

SWEET THINGS

This may seem a bit old fashioned – and well it might as it actually came from a Robert Carrier recipe card – but it is a lovely end to a meal. I like to make mine with really good aged dark rum as opposed to a thin flavourless white one. We changed it slowly, probably adding more booze and aromatic spices... I usually do.

RUM BABA

150g currants

100ml dark aged rum, plus more to soak and serve

240ml whole milk

5 tsp dried yeast

6 tsp caster sugar, plus 150g

pinch of salt

9 eggs

900g plain flour, sifted

375g unsalted butter, softened, in knobs

3 tbsp sultanas

3 star anise

1 cinnamon stick

Soak the currants in a few tablespoons of rum for an hour or so. Warm the milk to about blood temperature and add the yeast, the 6 tsp sugar and the salt.

In a food mixer with a dough hook, mix the milk and yeast mixture together with the eggs. Add half the flour. Cover with cling film and leave to prove for one hour in a warm place. Add the rest of the flour and work until smooth.

Now place the butter on top of the dough, cover and prove for another hour. Add the currants and their rum, then knead again until the butter is incorporated. Add the sultanas and shape into small dariole moulds (filling each two-thirds full). Leave to prove for 20 minutes while you preheat the oven to 180°C/350°F/gas mark 4. Bake for 20 minutes.

Meanwhile, make the syrup. Dissolve the remaining 150g sugar in 200ml water and the rum, add the star anise and cinnamon and cook for about five minutes over a medium heat. When the babas are ready, remove them from the moulds and put into a large tray. Pour over the syrup. Serve with whipped cream, splashing a little raw rum on each one.

I love Persian rice puddings and we often make a version at Dock Kitchen. You can finish this off with different things... we usually sprinkle it with pomegranate seeds or blood oranges, pistachios, dates or almonds. Anything delicious and exotic.

PERSIAN RICE PUDDING

1 litre whole milk

100g caster sugar

1 cinnamon stick

1 tsp orange flower water

finely grated zest of 2 oranges

finely grated zest of 1 unwaxed lemon

1 vanilla pod, split and seeds scraped out

1 tbsp cardamom seeds, finely crushed

100g risotto rice, washed well

200ml double cream

2 egg yolks

pinch of saffron threads, crushed in your fingers

8 dates

pinch of dried rose petals

Combine the milk, sugar, cinnamon stick, orange flower water, orange and lemon zest, vanilla pod and seeds, cardamom and rice in a large, heavy-based saucepan set over a medium heat. Bring to a boil, then reduce the heat right down. Cook for 45 minutes, stirring occasionally, or until the rice is completely soft. Be careful not to let the rice catch on the bottom of the pan, especially when it gets thick when it's almost ready.

Remove from the heat, whisk half the cream with the egg yolks, then stir this into the hot rice with the saffron and dates and set aside to cool completely.

Whip the remaining cream until thick, then stir it into the rice. Chill until cold. To serve, remove the cinnamon stick and vanilla pod, spoon the rice into bowls and sprinkle with rose petals and whatever else you have chosen.

I love to make this when the raspberries arrive and the Amalfi lemons are still tasting good. Try to buy good lemons, I find rough-skinned large European fruits to be the best.

LEMON CURD WITH RASPBERRIES AND SHORTBREAD

SERVES 6

For the shortbread

300g unsalted butter

350g plain flour

pinch of salt

115g caster sugar

For the lemon curd and raspberries

finely grated zest and juice of 7 unwaxed lemons

350g caster sugar

300g unsalted butter

6 whole eggs and 9 egg yolks

3 punnets of raspberries

For the shortbread, rub the butter and flour together into coarse crumbs, add the salt and sugar then knead briefly to bring together. Shape into a cylinder and wrap in cling film. Chill for an hour.

Preheat the oven to 180°C/350°F/gas mark 4. Cut the shortbread into 1cm rounds, then bake for 20 minutes. Remove and cool on a wire rack.

To make the lemon curd, heat the lemon zest, juice, sugar and butter in a medium saucepan. Whisk the eggs and yolks slightly to break them up. When the butter has melted, whisk in the eggs and continue cooking over a medium heat, stirring all the time, until the mixture is thick, less transparent and coats the back of a wooden spoon. As soon as it has thickened, remove from the pan into a jug (if you don't get it out of the pan the mixture will overcook and curdle).

Preheat the grill to full heat. Pour the mixture into six small ovenproof glasses or ramekins. Grill until there are large black spots on the curd. Eat with the raspberries, crème fraîche and a piece of shortbread.

This is a variation of a classic almond tart we often make. Sometimes we fill the tart with quarters of quince that we have slowly boiled in sugar syrup. We buy very expensive hazelnuts from Piedmonte and it seems like money well spent as they are truly delicious. Spanish and French hazelnuts can also be very good, though the most important thing is that they must not have started to turn rancid, as is often the case.

PEAR HAZELNUT AND ROSEMARY TART

SERVES 12–14

For the pastry

350g plain flour, sifted

100g icing sugar, sifted

225g unsalted butter

pinch of salt

3 egg yolks

For the filling

200g blanched hazelnuts, toasted

100g blanched almonds

250g unsalted butter

250g caster sugar

3 eggs

4 large pears (perhaps comice)

1 tsp demerara sugar

1 vanilla pod, split lengthways

75ml eau de vie, grappa or marc

2 sprigs of rosemary

In a food processor, pulse-blend the flour, icing sugar, butter and salt until coarse crumbs form. Add the egg yolks and pulse until the mixture begins to come together, turn it out and quickly knead a little to bind. Shape into two rounds, wrap in cling film and chill for a couple of hours.

Coarsely grind the nuts and remove from the machine. Blend the butter and caster sugar together, return the nuts followed by the eggs, then blend until well mixed. Peel the pears, halve them and remove the core. In a bowl, mix the pears with the brown sugar, vanilla seeds scraped from the pod and the eau de vie.

Preheat the oven to 160°C/325°F/gas mark 3. Grate the pastry into a 32cm tart tin and push into the sides and roughly down into the base (you might only use half the pastry but you can freeze the rest). Freeze for 10 minutes or so, then bake for 15 minutes until pale brown and firm to the touch. Cool for a few minutes, then spread the nut mixture into the shell. Push the pears in, then push the sprigs of rosemary in around the pears. Bake for 45 minutes to an hour, until browned, delicious looking and not too soft.

When the great Nigel Slater came to Dock Kitchen he ate this apple tart and pronounced it (no doubt over-generously) to be the best he had tried. It requires what I always think of as the long, hard task of making puff pastry, which in reality is not actually that hard but does take a while. It's always worth it though. Be sure to use the best quality butter you can find in the pastry, to ensure that your labour has been worthwhile.

APPLE TART

SERVES 10

For the puff pastry

500g unsalted butter

500g strong white flour, sifted, plus more to dust

pinch of sea salt

1 tbsp lemon juice

For the filling

6 sharp, sweet apples

juice of 1 lemon

150g unsalted butter

4 tbsp demerara sugar

2 egg yolks

To make the puff pastry, mix one-third of the butter with the flour and salt, add 250ml water and the lemon juice then mix into a firm dough. Push into a square, then wrap in cling film. Leave in the fridge for around an hour.

Once it has rested, roll the dough out on a lightly floured surface into a rectangle 5–10mm thick then, in a plastic bag or between two pieces of greaseproof paper, beat the remaining butter with a rolling pin into a rectangle a little bit smaller than half the rectangle of dough. Lay the butter on the dough, leaving a space at the end. Fold the unbuttered half over the butter and fold the edges over to make a parcel. Push together and pat into a square, wrap in cling film and allow to rest in the fridge for at least 15 minutes.

Once the dough has rested, roll it out into a rectangle, rolling in the opposite direction to the first fold. When the pastry is about 1cm thick, fold both ends in, one over the other, the centre third covered by the two outer thirds. Push together, pat into a square and allow to rest in the fridge for 15 minutes. Repeat twice more, then rest it in the fridge for at least another hour before you use it.

Preheat the oven to 180°C/350°F/gas mark 4. Roll the pastry out into a thin sheet and lay flat on a baking tray. Prick with a fork, leaving a 5cm margin all around the edge. Peel, core and very thinly slice the apples and toss them with the lemon. Melt the butter gently with the brown sugar, remove from the heat and stir in the egg yolks, add this mixture to the lemony sliced apples, then spread the apples in one layer over the pastry.

Bake for 12–15 minutes. Eat still warm, with ice cream if you are really feeling indulgent.

I love loganberries but, in their absence, raspberries will do. At other times of the year, this pudding is lovely with poached damsons or with roast figs.

ELDERFLOWER BUTTERMILK PUDDING WITH LOGANBERRIES

SERVES 8

4 sheets of leaf gelatine

350ml buttermilk

50g caster sugar, plus 4 tbsp more

250ml double cream

100ml good-quality elderflower cordial

200g loganberries

100ml eau de vie or grappa

Soak the gelatine in a bowl of cold water for a few minutes until soft, then squeeze the excess water from the soft leaves. Bring 100ml of the buttermilk to a boil with the 50g sugar. When the sugar has dissolved, remove from the heat and stir in the gelatine until dissolved. Leave to cool, then whisk into the cream with the rest of the buttermilk and the elderflower cordial. Pour into a ceramic tray or small moulds and leave to set in the fridge for two to three hours, or overnight.

Stir the loganberries with the remaining 4 tbsp sugar and the eau de vie. Spoon out the buttermilk pudding and serve with the boozy loganberries

You can vary the fruit, use whatever you like the look of at the market or, better still, what you have in the garden. I never include strawberries as I hate their texture in the mixture. Summer pudding is a brilliant English high summer dessert. Rose at River Café used to make a version with red wine. It was brilliant, I try to make a similar occasionally at Dock Kitchen.

RED WINE SUMMER PUDDING

SERVES 6–8

250g caster sugar, or to taste

1 vanilla pod, split lengthways

1 bottle light red wine

3 punnets of raspberries

2 punnets of blackcurrants, picked from the stalks

3 peaches, roughly chopped

1 small stale loaf of sourdough bread, crusts removed, very thinly sliced

Put the sugar, vanilla and 200ml water to heat in a large pan. Boil until the sugar starts to brown a little. When lightly golden, add the wine and reduce by half. Add the fruit, cook for five minutes, then taste the mixture. You may need to add more sugar depending on how acidic the fruit was.

Line a large pudding bowl with the bread. Pour in the fruit mixture and cover the top with a 'lid' of more bread. Put a plate on the top and then a weight, leave to cool, then put in the fridge overnight. Turn out and serve with pouring cream or crème fraîche.

I serve these little fried ravioli – called *sebadas* in Sardinia – with a glass of mirtillo, or a little bowl of special Sardinian bitter honey, though chestnut honey or any dark, strong honey would work well.

SARDINIAN CHESTNUT HONEY AND RICOTTA RAVIOLI

SERVES 6

200g fresh ricotta (ideally sheep's or buffalo's)

2 tbsp finely chopped candied peel

1 tsp orange flower water

75g icing sugar, or to taste, plus more to serve

For the dough

850g '00' flour

1 egg

125ml olive oil, plus more to deep-fry

To make the dough, place the flour in a pile on your work surface. Make a well in the centre and add the egg, olive oil and some warm water. Mix and add more water until you have a soft, almost sticky dough, kneading until glossy. You will need a total of 150-200ml water. Rest for about 30 minutes while you prepare the ricotta.

Mix the ricotta with the candied fruit, flower water and sugar. Taste, adding more sugar if you think it needs it.

Take half the dough and, using a pasta machine, roll it out into two long strips. Blob tablespoons of ricotta in two lines half the way along each strip of pasta about 10cm away from each other. Brush or spray with a little water, then fold the other half of the pasta over the top. Push down with your hands to make little parcels and then cut out with a ravioli or pizza cutter, or with a knife. Check each parcel is completely sealed by squeezing all around the edge with your fingers.

Heat a large saucepan with a couple of inches of cooking olive oil until a tiny drop of water fizzles and spits, but the oil must not be smoking (it should be at about 170°C/340°F if you have a thermometer). Fry the sebadas a few at a time. Remove when puffed up and golden, place on kitchen paper and dust with icing sugar. Serve with a little honey or a glass of mirtillo.

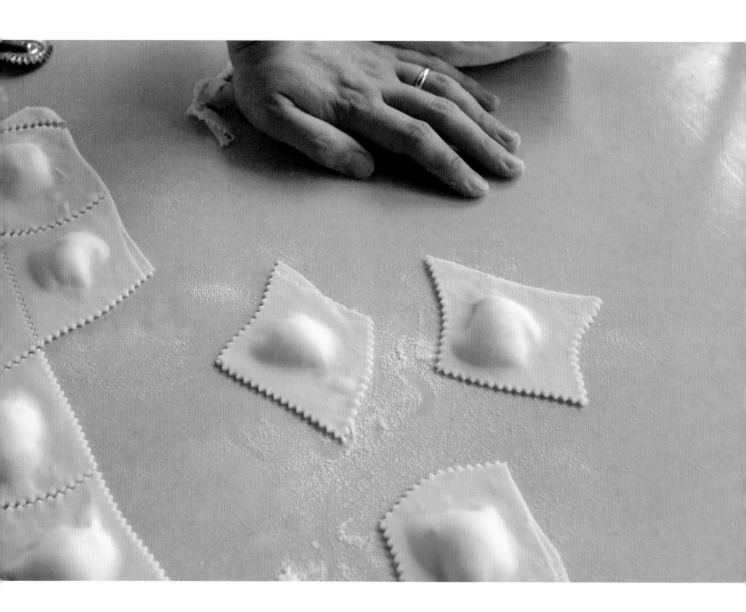

This is a brilliant tart from Naples. A classic to be made at Easter, I always include it in Easter menus and it is a lovely gift for someone in the spring. I would make it all year as I love it so much, but somehow it's nicer when you only make it for a few weeks... you get the feeling of occasion and excitement that you don't get if you make something very often.

PASTILLERA NAPOLITANA

For the pastry

350g plain flour, sifted, plus more to dust

225g unsalted butter

100g icing sugar

3 egg yolks

For the filling

300g farro

1 litre whole milk, plus more if needed

1 vanilla pod

1 cinnamon stick

a few pieces of lemon zest

200g caster sugar

3 whole eggs

200g ricotta

150g candied fruit or peel

50ml orange flower water

Soak the farro for the filling in water for a few hours.

In a blender, pulse-blend the flour, butter and icing sugar until it resembles crumbs. Add the egg yolks and pulse a little more, turn out the pastry, then knead very briefly to bring it together. Wrap in cling film and chill for a couple of hours.

Boil the farro in the milk with the vanilla, cinnamon, lemon zest and half the sugar. It will take about 40 minutes to go soft (depending on how long it was soaked for). You may need to add more milk if it reduces too much. When soft, drain off the excess liquid and set aside to cool.

Preheat the oven to 160°C/325°F/gas mark 3. Roll out two-thirds of the pastry on a lightly floured work surface and push it into a 26cm tart tin. Spike the base a few times with a fork and put in the freezer for 10 minutes. Bake for 15 minutes, until light brown.

Using an electric whisk, whisk the eggs with the remaining sugar fast for five minutes. Stir in the ricotta, candied fruit or peel and orange flower water. Add the farro and stir to combine. Pour into the baked tart shell.

Roll out the remainder of the pastry on a lightly floured work surface, cut it into strips then lay on top in a lattice shape. Bake for a further 45 minutes, until light brown and firm to the touch.

This is one of my favourite chocolate cakes. Though it is based on my friend Claire Ptak from Violet Cake's recipe for prune and armagnac chocolate cake, we switched the fruit and the alcohol. Feel free to revert to the original.

CHOCOLATE, APRICOT, BRANDY AND ALMOND CAKE

SERVES 10

300g unsalted butter, plus more for the tin

180g dried apricots, chopped

60ml brandy

360g good-quality dark chocolate, broken into pieces

9 eggs, separated

150g caster sugar

225g ground almonds

Preheat the oven to 150°C/300°F/gas mark 2. Butter the base and sides of a 25cm springform cake tin and line with baking parchment.

Soak the apricots in the brandy.

Melt the chocolate and butter in a stainless-steel or glass bowl over a pan of simmering water (make sure the base of the bowl does not touch the water).

Whisk the egg yolks with 100g of the sugar until light and pale. Add the apricots, brandy and almonds to the egg yolk mixture, followed by the chocolate. Stir gently to combine.

Whisk the egg whites with the remaining sugar, then fold into the chocolate mixture.

Bake for 30–40 minutes; make sure it's still a little wobbly in the centre when it comes out of the oven. Cool in the tin before you turn it out. Serve with crème fraîche.

Bergamot is a citrus that looks like a round lemon and an oil made from the zest is used to flavour Earl Grey tea. It's an intriguing taste. We buy bergamot during the winter from natoora.co.uk, but you could also use a combination of orange and lemon zest – perhaps 2 oranges, 1 lemon or 1 tsp orange flower water – if you can't find fresh bergamot. You will need a madeleine tray. Serve these with fresh fruit or a light jam.

BERGAMOT MADELEINES

135g unsalted butter, plus more for the tray

2 tbsp honey

3 large eggs

130g caster sugar

135g self-raising flour, sifted, plus more for the tray

finely grated zest of 3 bergamots, juice of 1

Melt the butter with the honey in a small saucepan over a low heat. Set aside to cool. Whisk the eggs with the sugar in an electric mixer for 10 minutes or so, until the mixture triples in size. Fold in the flour, zest, juice and the butter and honey mixture. Leave to rest for three hours, or overnight in the fridge.

Preheat the oven to 190°C/375°F/gas mark 5. Butter a madeleine tray, then dust with flour and tip off the excess. (You may need to cook these in two batches, depending on the size of your tray.) Fill the moulds two-thirds full, then bake for 10 minutes until golden brown and firm to the touch. Let cool until just warm, then eat with tea or pink champagne.

We make this all year, with thinly sliced apples, white peaches, apricots, pears, grapes, rhubarb... almost anything, varying the amount of sugar depending on the fruit and how tart it is. Sometimes we put crushed almonds on the fruit, sometimes brown sugar and melted butter. This version is with nespole (the Italian name for Japanese loquats). You see them for sale in Middle Eastern shops in the late spring.

FRUIT CROSTATA

MAKES 2 LARGE CROSTATA

370g unsalted butter

500g plain flour, sifted, plus more to dust

4 tbsp caster sugar, plus 200g

½ tsp salt

1kg nespole, stones removed

100g blanched almonds, toasted and roughly chopped

Rub one-third of the butter into the flour, the 4 tbsp of sugar and salt until it resembles crumbs, then mix in the remaining butter. Do not mix in well, the butter lumps need to remain pea-sized and, when you roll out the pastry, it's good to have big flakes of butter. Add 4 tbsp iced water bit by bit until the pastry comes together. Knead by dropping the pastry through your hands, not pushing it together. Rest, wrapped in cling film, for at least two hours in the fridge.

Now roll out two discs on a lightly floured work surface, each about 6mm thick. Put the fruit in the centre, leaving a margin of 10cm around the edge of both, sprinkle over the 200g sugar and the almonds, then fold the pastry over the fruit, overlapping it and pinching to make a free-form crust. Rest again in the fridge until the pastry is firm. Preheat the oven to 200°C/400°F/gas mark 6.

Cook for about 25 minutes, until light brown.

DAMSON The damson season is short and I always greet it with great excitement. They are so intensely flavoured that they make a really fabulous ice cream. It is very easy to make as it doesn't include a custard.

QUINCE I cooked this ice cream for my first supper club – way before they were called 'pop-ups' – in 2006 with my great friends Joe and Blanche. It is a delicious, fragrant ice cream we make often during the season.

DAMSON ICE CREAM

SERVES 4

500g damsons

200g caster sugar, or to taste

250ml double cream

250ml natural yogurt

Rinse the damsons, then bring to a boil with 100ml water in a stainless-steel pan. It probably won't seem like enough water, but it'll be OK. Reduce the heat so the damsons simmer gently for 10 minutes, until the skins have burst and you have a quantity of deep purple juice.

Push the fruit through a fine sieve with a wooden spoon, pushing until you have nothing left but stones. Return to the heat with the sugar and heat to dissolve. Leave the purée to cool. Stir in the cream and yogurt, taste to check the amount of sugar (remembering that, when frozen, sweetness is less pronounced).

Churn in an ice cream machine, or freeze in a tray for about four hours, whisking every 30 minutes.

QUINCE ICE CREAM

SERVES 6

4 quinces

350g caster sugar

1 vanilla pod

½ a 37.5cl bottle of moscato d'asti

400ml double cream or crème fraîche

juice of ½ lemon

sea salt

Place the whole quinces in a pan with the sugar, vanilla and wine. Cover with foil and cook on a very low heat for three and a half to four hours until they're really soft and a burnt-orange colour. Cool, then push through a sieve.

When cold, add the cream or crème fraîche, lemon and salt. Place in an ice cream machine and churn.

This recipe is based on a classic burnt caramel ice cream, the addition of salt adds a whole new dimension. I am a fully paid-up subscriber to the quite trendy taste of salt and caramel, pioneered by some of the country's best chocolate makers.

SALT AND CARAMEL ICE CREAM

SERVES 6

500ml whole milk

500ml double cream

2 vanilla pods, split, seeds scraped out

10 egg yolks

250g caster sugar

sea salt

Heat the milk, cream and vanilla seeds together gently for 10 minutes until just about to boil. Whisk the egg yolks with half the sugar. Pour the hot milk and cream over the egg yolks, whisking as you do.

Return the egg and milk mixture to the rinsed-out pan and cook, stirring with a wooden spoon, until thick enough to coat the back of a spoon and too hot to comfortably hold your hand in the mixture. It should be thick and velvety. When it is, pour it into a mixing bowl.

Put the remaining sugar in a pan with about the same amount of water and cook over a medium heat until dark brown and smoky. While still burning hot, carefully pour the burnt sugar on to the cooling custard, stirring with a whisk the whole time until any lumps of burnt sugar have dissolved. Add salt to taste, then leave to cool. Churn in an ice cream machine.

You can vary the alcohol, though if you don't use mezcal, and use brandy or whisky instead, you should ditch the chillies and cinnamon and replace them with vanilla. I use an aged, smoky mezcal from the south of Mexico but a good tequila would do. This is a brilliantly grown-up tasting ice. Only serve a small portion as it is really intense. *Nieve* means snow in Spanish.

CHOCOLATE AND MEZCAL NIEVE

250g caster sugar

2.5cm piece of cinnamon stick

1 dried smoked Mexican chilli (chipotle or pasilla de Oaxaca)

150g cocoa

100ml mezcal or tequila

Melt the sugar with 750ml of water, the cinnamon and chilli. Bring to a boil, reduce the heat, then simmer for two minutes to stabilise the sugar.

Pour in the cocoa slowly, whisking as you do, and simmer, whisking occasionally, for another five minutes.

Leave to cool, then add the alcohol.

Churn in an ice cream machine, or freeze in a freezer tray, stirring every 30 minutes until frozen. It will take about three hours, depending on your tray and the temperature of your freezer.

Try to find some really good-quality candied fruit. Often Spanish or Portuguese shops have delicious figs and oranges.

TUTTI FRUTTI ICE CREAM

500ml whole milk

500ml double cream

1 vanilla pod, split, seeds scraped out

10 egg yolks

150g caster sugar

2 tbsp amaretto

200g very good-quality mixed candied peel, chopped

Heat the milk, cream and vanilla seeds together gently for 10 minutes until just about to boil. Whisk the egg yolks with the sugar. Pour the hot milk and cream over the egg yolks, whisking as you do.

Return the egg and milk mixture back to the cleaned-out pan and cook, stirring with a wooden spoon, until thick enough to coat the back of a spoon and too hot to comfortably hold your hand in the mixture. It should be thick and velvety. As soon as it is, pour it out into a bowl, add the amaretto and leave to cool. Churn in an ice cream machine, stirring in the chopped candied fruit at the end of the process.

Blood oranges vary a lot in sweetness as the season progresses, so this could need double the amount of sugar or even just a pinch.

CAMPARI AND BLOOD ORANGE GRANITA

SERVES 4

juice of 6 blood oranges

100ml Campari

100g caster sugar, or to taste

Mix the orange juice with the Campari. Add sugar to taste; don't forget that it will taste a little less sweet when frozen.

Transfer to a freezer container. Freeze until solid (about three hours depending on the temperature of the freezer and the amount of sugar used).

Pare off curls of granita with a large spoon and serve in elegant glasses.

THE

NEW BASICS

SPICE MIXES

Having a few spice mixes up your sleeve is really useful. It's like having magic powders, each of which makes things taste truly delicious. We have developed these recipes over the last few years at the restaurant; we make lots of different ones but we find that these are the most useful.

BAGHDAD BHARAT This can be scaled up or down according to how much you need. It's a really useful mix, you can use it to flavour beans, lentils or any kind of grain as well as for roasting meat, especially lamb. Don't worry if you don't have one of the ingredients, it generally works pretty well anyway.

Makes a small jarful

60g black peppercorns

30g paprika

10g cayenne

70g cumin seeds

40g turmeric

60g coriander seeds

35g cloves

40g cinnamon sticks

40g whole nutmeg

50g dried limes

20g cardamom seeds

10g ground ginger

LEBANESE SEVEN SPICE We vary this, sometimes adding fenugreek instead of cumin. It's an incredibly useful spice for Middle Eastern cooking. Used almost like pepper, you can season a lamb chop with it, or add it to vegetables or any pilaf. It has a high quantity of nutmeg and cloves, which gives it a brilliantly intense fragrance.

Makes a small jarful

150g coriander seeds

130g cumin seeds

120g allspice berries

150g cinnamon sticks

40g cloves

180g black peppercorns

40g whole nutmeg

In both cases, grind all the whole spices separately in a mortar and pestle or spice grinder, then mix together. Store in a jar with a tight-fitting lid.

TOASTED SRI LANKAN MASALA Another very useful spice mix. I mostly add this to dhal or roasted cashew nuts, it brings beautiful, warm toasted flavours to a dish.

Makes enough for a few batches of dhal

30g coriander seeds

20g cumin seeds

20g fennel seeds

10g fenugreek seeds

15g cinnamon sticks

10g cardamom seeds

1 large, mild dried chilli

10g black peppercorns

Roast the spices in a large dry frying pan until the mixture is hot but not yet popping or smoking. Grind them finely in a spice grinder or mortar and pestle. Store in a jar with a tight-fitting lid.

CHAAT This spice mix is complex and tasty. It is very good just sprinkled on a sliced tomato or fried chickpeas or potatoes.

Makes a small jarful

30g cardamom seeds

20g rose petals

20g fennel seeds

30g coriander seeds

10g cloves

30g cinnamon sticks

30g mustard seeds

20g ground ginger

10g turmeric

1 scant tsp chilli powder

40g amchur

5g asafoetida

Grind the whole spices separately, then mix them with everything else. Store in an airtight container.

BREAD

There are some breads you can make well without proper bread ovens and loads of space. Generally flatbreads. These days, most of our breads at the restaurant are sourdough, as I'm not mad keen on the taste of commercial yeast. We switched to natural levain, which has a lovely wholesome taste and a wonderful acidity. At home, however, I use dried yeast and the results are perfectly good.

For the toast recipes we buy a southern Italian semolina bread, or a coarse sourdough; generally the French breads are not as well suited to eating with olive oil, they seem much happier with butter.

MOROCCAN SEMOLINA LOAVES These are lovely soft breads, perfect to eat with Moroccan food. You see people carrying them on wooden trays through the streets to the communal ovens in Moroccan towns; these are the same ovens that heat the water for the communal baths and also that cook the tangias. Tangias are beautiful coarse terracotta pots (see the photo on the previous page), that get buried in the ash of the oven for the meat to cook overnight.

Makes 3 loaves

20g fresh yeast, or 2 tsp dried yeast

1kg fine semolina (the kind for making pasta)

100ml olive oil

2 tsp fine salt

Crumble the yeast into about 100ml of lukewarm water and mix with your fingers to a smooth brown liquid. Add a little of the semolina and set aside somewhere warm for about 10 minutes. Mix the yeasty mixture into the remaining semolina with the olive oil and salt. Add warm water until you have a thick dough that sticks to your hands. Turn the dough out on to your work surface and knead it until it becomes quite glossy and less sticky, adding a little more semolina if it is still sticking to your hands. Put in a bowl and cover with cling film. Leave to prove somewhere warm for about 40 minutes.

Shape the dough into three round, flat loaves and leave to prove on a well-floured baking tray covered in a damp tea towel for around an hour. Preheat the oven to 200°C/400°F/gas mark 6. Bake for 45 minutes, until hollow-sounding when knocked on the bottom.

PLAIN WHITE CHAPATI

Both versions make 12 small chapati

350ml warm water

1 tsp fine salt

1 tbsp olive oil

600g strong white flour

BROWN CHAPATI

350ml warm water

1 tsp fine salt

1 tbsp olive oil

400g strong white flour

200g wholemeal bread flour, sifted

Mix the water, salt and olive oil into the flour. Knead well until glossy and stretchy, it will take about 10 minutes. Leave to rest for about 30 minutes, then shape into little balls and roll out into very thin discs, bigger than a CD, smaller than a LP. Heat a flat large frying pan and place in a disc of dough. Once it changes from glossy to dull, translucent to opaque, flip it over and then, after a few seconds, flip it out directly on to the gas flame. The flames will make the chapati puff up. Remove it from the heat and cover with a napkin while you make the rest. Be careful not to burn yourself or set a bread on fire. Just a few seconds on the flame should be enough.

AMRITSARI KULCHA (STUFFED ROTI) These

delicious breads take a while, but it is a lovely process. They are flaky, like a croissant filled with spiced potato.

Makes about 8

For the dough

400g strong white flour, plus more to dust

3 tbsp sunflower oil

200ml water

3 tbsp clarified butter or ghee

For the filling

2 waxy potatoes, peeled

sea salt

2 tbsp sunflower oil

1 tsp cumin seeds

2 fresh mild green chillies, finely chopped

2 spring onions, finely chopped

½ bunch of coriander, chopped

First put the potatoes on to boil in salted water for the potato filling.

In a large bowl, mix the flour, oil and water together. Knead until you have a glossy, slightly sticky dough. Shape into slightly larger than golf ball-sized spheres and leave to rest on a tray wrapped in cling film.

Once the potatoes are cooked, drain them, then mash them up a bit with a wooden spoon and set aside. Heat a large frying pan over a high heat, add the sunflower oil for the filling and, when hot, sprinkle in the cumin. When the cumin starts to crackle, add the green chilli, spring onions and coriander. Reduce the heat, season well with salt and cook for about five minutes, until the spring onion is soft. Add the potatoes and stir to incorporate all the onion mixture into the potato. Set aside to cool.

Melt the clarified butter in a small saucepan. On a floured surface, roll out a ball of dough as thinly as you possibly can into a disc about 30cm across (don't worry if it has some small holes in), spread with a bit of clarified butter then put a couple of tablespoons of the potato mixture into the middle (spread the potato out as much as you can). Fold two of the sides up over the potato, turn it over and fold the other two over to make a small square parcel. Press down firmly to make a disc around the size of a CD and set aside. Repeat the process until you have no dough or potato left. At this point you can leave them in the fridge overnight.

When you are ready to cook them, preheat the oven to its highest setting and bake them on a heavy roasting tray. When they are done, scrunch and tear them a little bit inside a clean dry cloth to separate the layers.

GRILLED YEASTED FLATBREAD We make this bread every day, generally cooking it in the tandoor oven, though it also works well on a griddle pan.

Makes about 6

| 1 tbsp dried yeast |
| about 650ml warm water |
| 1.2kg strong white flour |
| 2 tsp fine salt |

Soak the yeast in about 10ml of the warm water, mixing to a smooth liquid.

Add the yeasty water and the remaining water to the flour and salt and mix until all the liquid is incorporated but the mixture is lumpy. Let sit for 10 minutes.

Now knead for five to 10 minutes. Prove, covered in cling film, for one hour. Shape into four balls and prove on a tray or work surface covered with a damp cloth.

Preheat the oven to the hottest setting or heat a cast-iron griddle pan on the hob. Roll the balls into large flatbreads, the same size as the tray or griddle. Griddle or bake for three to five minutes.

PITTA BREAD This recipe was developed by Lughan, my old head chef; he is a lovely cook and an excellent baker. It has a quite a few stages, but is simple enough and yields excellent results.

Makes enough bread for 12

| 1 tbsp dried yeast |
| about 650ml warm water |
| 150g unsalted butter |
| 1.2kg strong white flour |
| 2 tsp fine salt |

Soak the yeast in about 10ml of the warm water, mixing to a smooth liquid.

Rub the butter into the flour as if you were making pastry, until it forms very fine crumbs. Add the yeasty water, the remaining water and the salt and mix until all the liquid is incorporated but the mixture is lumpy. Let sit for 10 minutes.

Now knead for five to 10 minutes. Prove, covered in cling film, for one hour. Shape into golf ball-sized pieces and prove on a tray or work surface covered with a damp cloth.

Preheat the oven to the hottest setting and put a heavy baking tray or pizza stone into the oven to get hot. Roll each piece of dough into pitta shapes about 4mm thick, then prove for a few more minutes. Bake them directly on the hot tray or stone for about three minutes, until slightly puffed up and lightly browned.

opposite, from top Lebanese Seven Spice (see page 182); Plain White Chapati (see page 183)

PICKLES AND CHUTNEYS

It is always worth making a few pickles to keep in the larder, you don't need to be a paid-up member of the WI to wield a preserving pan. Just a spoonful will make dishes come alive. See the chicken recipe on page 66 for an example of how useful they can be.

FRESH PINEAPPLE CHUTNEY This keeps for about a week in the fridge. It adds a bit of sunshine and zing to any simple, earthy Indian dishes.

Makes a large bowlful

1 pineapple

4 tbsp sunflower oil

1 tsp mustard seeds

small handful of curry leaves, picked from stems

¼ tsp chilli powder

small pinch of asafoetida

½ tsp crushed black pepper

juice of 2 limes

Peel the pineapple and chop into 1cm dice, discarding the core. Heat a large wide pan, add the oil, then the mustard seeds, followed by the curry leaves. Allow to crackle, then add the other spices, followed immediately by the pineapple. Season with salt and add the lime. Cook for five minutes over a high heat, then transfer to a bowl and leave to cool. Eat at room temperature.

PICKLED SQUASH This is a great thing to have kicking around. A few slices with a piece of ham, some pâté or any cold meat makes a perfect lunch.

Makes a large bowlful

1 small, ripe squash (acorn, onion or butternut)

1 tsp mustard seeds

1 tsp coriander seeds

10 bay leaves

1 tsp sea salt

3 tbsp sugar

1 litre good red wine vinegar

Thinly slice your squash. Put all the other ingredients into a pan and bring to a boil. Sterelise a jar and push the squash into it. Pour over the hot pickling liquid and seal. Eat after two weeks and before three months.

LEMON PICKLE This recipe came from a funny little cookery book I picked up in Kerala, we make it often at Dock Kitchen and have adapted it a lot. I like to have a jar in the fridge all the time in case anything needs a bit of a spicy sour kick. This makes a lot, but you can easily halve the quantities. Try to find really good lemons (we use lovely ones from Amalfi), it makes a big difference. They must be unwaxed and probably will be better if organic.

Makes a massive jarful

25 unwaxed lemons

140ml oil (I often use olive oil but sunflower might be better)

2 tbsp mustard seeds

large pinch of asafoetidaa

1 tbsp fenugreek seeds

2 tsp turmeric

60g garlic cloves, halved, green sprouts removed

60g fresh root ginger, peeled and very thinly sliced into strips

18 large mild green chillies, split in half (take the seeds and white part out to make it milder)

1 tsp chilli powder

250g coarse salt

Wash the lemons, cut each into eight pieces and steam them until completely soft.

Heat a large wide pan and add the oil. When hot, add the mustard seeds and, when they crackle, add the rest of the ingredients except the lemons and salt. Cook briskly for five minutes, then add the lemons and salt. Mix well and transfer to a sterile container. Keep in the fridge if possible. Leave for a month before eating.

INDEX

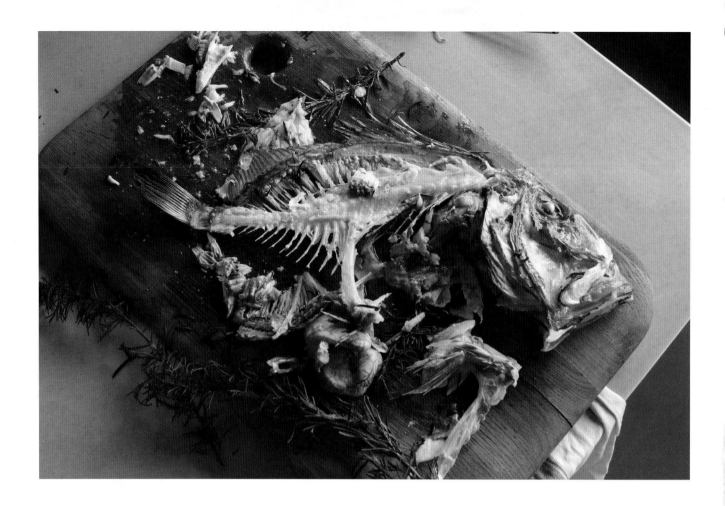

ACKNOWLEDGEMENTS

I would like to thank everyone at Dock Kitchen past and present, particularly Alex, Lughan, Matthew, Aoibhenn and Richard for working so hard and cooking so brilliantly that I could take the time to write. Nick and Tom and Mark for making it all run a bit more smoothly. Tom Dixon for helping it all happen. Lawrence and Toby for making this book look so great and Lucy for being a patient, brilliant editor. Everyone at Quadrille, particularly Anne for being so wonderfully supportive. Mostly, of course, for my beautiful wife and son for being there with smiles when I need them.

700039455010